D1320842

NAVIES OF THE SECOND WORLD WAR

AMERICAN FLEET AND ESCORT DESTROYERS 2

H. T. LENTON

MACDONALD : LONDON

SBN 356 03123 3

First published in 1971 by
Macdonald & Co. (Publishers) Ltd.,
49 Poland Street, London, W.1.
Made and printed in Great Britain by
Waterlow and Sons Limited, London and Dunstable

"Gearing" class: **ABNER READ, AGERHOLM, ARNOLD J. ISBELL, BASILONE, BAUSSELL, BENNER, BORDELON, BRINKLEY BASS, BROWNSON, CARPENTER, CASTLE, CHARLES H. ROAN(i), CHARLES H. ROAN(ii), CHARLES P. CECIL, CHARLES R. WARE, CHEVALIER, CONE, CORRY, DAMATO, DENNIS J. BUCKLEY, DUNCAN, DYESS, EPPERSON, ERNEST G. SMALL, EUGENE A. GREENE, EVERETT F. LARSEN, EVERSOLE, FECHTELER, FISKE, FLOYD B. PARKES, FORREST ROYAL, FRANK KNOX, FRED T. BERRY, FURSE, GEARING, GEORGE K. MACKENZIE, GLENNON, GOODRICH, GURKE, GYATT, HAMNER, HANSON, HARWOOD, HAROLD J. ELLISON, HAWKINS, HENDERSON, HENRY W. TUCKER, HERBERT J. THOMAS, HIGBEE, HOEL, HOLDER, HOLLISTER, JAMES E. KYES, JOHN R. CRAIG, JOHNSTON, JOSEPH P. KENNEDY JR., KENNETH D. BAILEY, KEPPLER, LANSDALE, LEARY, LEONARD F. MASON, LLOYD THOMAS, McCAFFERY, McKEAN, MEREDITH, MYLES C. FOX, NEW, NEWMAN K. PERRY, NOA, NORRIS, O'HARE, ORLECK, OZBOURN, PERKINS, PERRY, POWER, RICH, RICHARD B. ANDERSON, RICHARD E. KRAUSS, ROBERT A. OWENS, ROBERT H. McCARD, ROBERT L. WILSON, ROGERS, ROWAN, RUPERTUS, SAMUEL B. ROBERTS, SARSFIELD, SEAMAN, SEYMOUR D. OWEN, SHELTON, SOUTHERLAND, STEINAKER, STICKEL, STRIBLING, THEODORE E. CHANDLER, TIMMERMAN, TURNER, VESOLE, VOGELGESANG, WARRINGTON, WILLIAM C. LAWE, WILLIAM M. WOOD, WILLIAM R. RUSH, WILTSIE, WITEK, WOODROW R. THOMPSON** and **FIFTY-ONE** unnamed vessels.

Except that a 14-foot section was added amidships to provide increased hull space, these vessels were otherwise similar to the "Allen M. Sumner" class, from which they could be distinguished by their wider spaced funnels.

While completing several units (*DD.805–808, 829–835* and *873–883*) had the forward bank of T.T. replaced by a tripod mast carrying long range AW.RDF to act as radar pickets, and most other units (*DD.710, 713–718, 763–765, 782–791, 817–835, 851–853* and *858–887*) had the after bank replaced by four 40 mm. A.A. (1 × 4) guns. In addition, the 3-inch/50 cal. A.A. began to replace the 40 mm. gun and was installed in a few units (*DD.788–790, 852, 853, 865, 868, 872* and *873*), while an ahead throwing A/S spigot mortar (Hedgehog) was fitted in most of the final vessels (*DD.851–853* and *858–887*).

3

Above: As completed the GEARING *lacked the after bank of T.T. and finally shipped an additional quadruple 40 mm. A.A. mounting in this position. Below: A tripod mast carrying long-range AW.RDF has replaced the forward bank of T.T. in the* SOUTHERLAND.

After the cessation of hostilities construction was cancelled on *DD.720, 721, 766* and *767* (all launched), *DD.768* and *769* (both laid down), and fifty-one other vessels, and while *Seaman* (*DD.791*) was completed she was never placed in service. Construction was also halted on *DD.719, 824, 825* and *828* which were finally completed in 1949 to modified designs as prototype A/S and escort destroyers.

Displacement:	2,425 tons (3,480 tons full load).
Dimensions:	383 (wl) 390½ except *DD.888* 389¾/*DD.765* 390¼/*DD.763* and *764* 390¾/*DD.890* 391 (oa) × 41 except *DD.766–769* 40¾ × 15½ (18¾ full load) feet.
Machinery:	Four Babcock & Wilcox except *DD.766–769, 782–791, 824, 862–872* and *887* Foster Wheeler boilers; two shafts; General Electric except *DD.710–712, 714, 715, 717, 718, 742, 743, 822, 823, 850–853, 859, 868–870, 879, 880* and *886* Westinghouse DR geared turbines S.H.P. 60,000 = 35 except *DD.851–853, 858–887* 34½ (32 full load) knots.
Bunkers and radius:	740 except *DD.824* 745/*DD.782–784, 817–823, 858–861, 873, 875* and *878–887* 745/ *DD.742, 865, 890* 720/*DD.710–721* 515 tons; 6,000 miles at 15 knots.
Armament:	Six 5-inch/38 cal. D.P. (3 × 2); six 3-inch/50 cal. A.A. (2 × 2 and 2 × 1), four 40 mm. A.A. (1 × 4) and eleven 20 mm. A.A. (11 × 1) in *DD.852, 853, 865, 868, 872* and *873* or four 3-inch/50 cal. A.A. (2 × 2), eight 40 mm. A.A. (1 × 4 and 2 × 2) and eleven 20 mm. A.A. (11 × 1) in *DD.788–790* or sixteen 40 mm. A.A. (3 × 4 and 2 × 2) and eight 20 mm. A.A. (8 × 1) in *DD.829–835*/ten 20 mm. A.A. (10 × 1) in *DD.710, 712–718, 720* and *721*/eleven 20 mm. A.A. (11 × 1) in *DD.763–769, 782–787, 791, 817– 823, 826, 828, 851, 858–864, 866, 867, 869–871* and *874–887* or twelve 40 mm. A.A. (2 × 4 and 2 × 2) and ten 20 mm. A.A. (10 × 1) in *DD.711, 836–843* and *845–850*/ eleven 20 mm. A.A. (11 × 1) in *DD.742, 743, 805–808* and *888–890*/fifteen 20 mm. A.A. (3 × 4 and 3 × 1) in *DD.844* guns; ten except *DD.710, 712–718, 720, 721, 763– 769, 782–791, 805–808, 817–823, 826, 828, 851–853, 858–873* and *884–887* five/*DD.829– 835* and *874–883* nil 21-inch (1/2 × 5) T.T.; one A/S spigot mortar (Hedgehog) in *DD. 851–853* and *858–887* only.
Complement:	336 except *DD.805–808, 817–853* and *858–890* 367.

Hull No.	Name	Builder	Launched	Fate
DD.710	Gearing	Federal Sbdg. (Kearny)	18.2.45	
DD.711	Eugene A. Greene (ii)	,,	18.3.45	DDR.711 (1952), DD.711 (1963).
DD.712	Gyatt (ii)	,,	15.4.45	DDG.1 (1955), DDG.712 (1956), DDG.1. (1957), DD.712 (1962; stricken 22/10/69 and scrapped.
DD.713	Kenneth D. Bailey (ii)	,,	17.6.44	DDR.713 (1953), DD.713 (1969).
DD.714	William R. Rush (ii)	,,	8.7.45	DDR.714 (1953), DD.714 (1963).
DD.715	William M. Wood (ii)	,,	29.7.45	DDR.715 (1953), DD.715 (1963).
DD.716	Wiltsie	,,	31.8.45	
DD.717	Theodore E. Chandler	,,	20.10.45	
DD.718	Hamner	,,	25.11.45	
DD.719	Epperson	,,	22.12.45	Completed Bath I.W., DDE.719 (1949), DD.719 (1962).

Both the HOLLISTER (*above*) and the SHELTON (*below*) have had the after bank of T.T. replaced by a quadruple 40 mm. A.A. mounting, and single 20 mm. with twin 20 mm. mountings. The forward 20 mm. gun has been suppressed, and the SHELTON has also had the 20 mm. guns at the stern omitted.

Hull No.	Name	Builder	Launched	Fate
DD.720	Castle	Federal Sbdg. (Kearny)	46	Cancelled 11/2/46 sold .... 29/8/55 and scrapped incomplete.
DD.721	Woodrow R. Thompson	,,	46	Cancelled 11/2/46, sold .... 29/8/55 and scrapped incomplete.
DD.742	Frank Knox	Bath I.W.	17.9.44	DDR.742 (1949), DD.742 (1969).
DD.743	Southerland	,,	5.10.44	DDR.743 (1949), DD.743 (1963).
DD.763	William C. Lawe (iii)	Bethlehem (San Francisco)	21.5.45	
DD.764	Lloyd Thomas (iii)	,,	5.10.45	DDK.764 (1949), DDE.764 (1950), DD.764 (1962).
DD.765	Keppler (iii)	,,	24.6.46	DDK.765 (1949), DDE.765 (1950), DD.765 (1962).
DD.766	Lansdale (ii)	,,	20.12.46	Cancelled 7/1/46, bow used to repair Floyd B. Parks (DD.884) 1956, sold ..../../59 and scrapped incomplete.
DD.767	Seymour D. Owen	,,	24.2.47	Cancelled 7/1/46, bow used to repair Ernest G. Small (DD.838) 1952, stricken 9/6/58 and scrapped incomplete.
DD.768	Hoel (ii)	,,	—	Cancelled 12/9/46 and scrapped on slip.
DD.769	Abner Read (ii)	,,	—	Cancelled 12/9/46 and scrapped on slip.

In HIGBEE (*above*) *and* TURNER (*below*) *both banks of T.T. have been replaced by a tripod mast carrying AW.RDF and an additional quadruple 40 mm. A.A. mounting.*

Hull No.	Name	Builder	Launched	Fate
DD.782	*Rowan (ii)*	Todd Pacific (Seattle)	29.12.44	
DD.783	*Gurke*	,,	15.2.45	
DD.784	*McKean*	,,	31.3.45	DDR.784 (1952), DD.784 (1963).
DD.785	*Henderson*	,,	28.5.45	
DD.786	*Richard B. Anderson*	,,	7.7.45	
DD.787	*James E. Kyes*	,,	4.8.45	
DD.788	*Hollister*	,,	9.10.45	
DD.789	*Eversole (ii)*	,,	8.1.46	
DD.790	*Shelton (iii)*	,,	8.3.46	
DD.791	*Seaman*	,,	20.5.46	Bow used to repair *Collett* (DD.730), stricken ../3/61 and scrapped.

Only the after bank of T.T. has been replaced by an additional quadruple 40 mm. A.A. mounting in STEINAKER (*above*) and CHARLES R. WARE (*below*).

Hull No.	Name	Builder	Launched	Fate
DD.805	*Chevalier (ii)*	Bath I.W.	29.10.44	DDR.805 (1949), DD.805 (1963).
DD.806	*Higbee*	,,	12.11.44	DDR.806 (1949), DD.806 (1963).
DD.807	*Benner (ii)*	,,	30.11.44	DDR.807 (1949), DD.807 (1963).
DD.808	*Dennis J. Buckley (ii)*	,,	20.12.44	DDR.808 (1949), DD.808 (1963).
DD.809	Unnamed	,,	—	Cancelled 12/8/45.
DD.810	Unnamed	,,	—	Cancelled 12/8/45.
DD.811	Unnamed	,,	—	Cancelled 12/8/45.
DD.812	Unnamed	,,	—	Cancelled 12/8/45.
DD.813	Unnamed	Bethlehem (Staten Island)	—	Cancelled 12/8/45.
DD.814	Unnamed	,,	—	Cancelled 12/8/45.
DD.815	*Charles H. Roan (i)*	Consolidated Steel Corp. (Orange)	—	Cancelled 12/8/45.
DD.816	Unnamed	,,	—	Cancelled 12/8/45.

Both banks of T.T. were omitted from the HAWKINS *but only the after set was replaced by a quadruple 40 mm. A.A. mounting.*

Hull No.	Name	Builder	Launched	Fate
DD.817	Corry (ii)	Consolidated Steel Corp. (Orange)	28.7.45	DDR.817 (1953), DD.817 (1963).
DD.818	New	,,	18.8.45	DDE.818 (1953), DD.818 (1962).
DD.819	Holder (ii)	,,	25.8.45	DDE.819 (1953), DD.819 (1962).
DD.820	Rich (ii)	,,	5.10.45	DDE.820 (1953), DD.820 (1962).
DD.821	Johnston (ii)	,,	19.10.45	
DD.822	Robert H. McCard	,,	9.11.45	
DD.823	Samuel B. Roberts (ii)	,,	30.11.45	Stricken 2/11/70 and scrapped.
DD.824	Basilone	,,	21.12.45	Completed Bethlehem (Quincy), DDE.824 (1949), DD.824 (1962).
DD.825	Carpenter	,,	28.12.45	Completed Newport News DDK. 825 (1949), DDE.825 (1950), DD.825 (1962).
DD.826	Agerholm	Bath I.W.	30.3.45	

Only the after bank of T.T. had been replaced in Cone (*above*), *while* Dyess (*below*) *lacked both sets and later has a tripod mast stepped amidships carrying AW.RDF.*

Hull No.	Name	Builder	Launched	Fate
DD.827	Robert A. Owens	Bath I.W.	15.7.46	Completed Newport News DDK. 827 (1949), DDE.827 (1950), DD.827 (1962).
DD.828	Timmerman	,,	19.5.51	EDD.828 (1949), AG.152 (1952); sold ..../../59 and scrapped.
DD.829	Myles C. Fox(ii)	,,	13.1.45	DDR.829 (1949), DD.829 (1964).
DD.830	Everett F. Larson (ii)	,,	28.1.45	DDR.830 (1949), DD.830 (1962).
DD.831	Goodrich	,,	25.2.45	DDR.831 (1949), DD.831 (1969).
DD.832	Hanson	,,	11.3.45	DDR.832 (1949), DD.832 (1963).
DD.833	Herbert J. Thomas	,,	25.3.45	DDR.833 (1949), DD.833 (1963).
DD.834	Turner (iii)	,,	8.4.45	DDR.834 (1949), DD.834 (1969); sold Southern Scrap Materials Co. (New Orleans) ../../70 & scrapped.
DD.835	Charles P. Cecil	,,	22.4.45	DDR.835 (1949), DD.835 (1963).
DD.836	George K. MacKenzie	,,	13.5.45	

The BASILONE (*above*) and ROBERT A. OWEN (*below*) as completed post-war and modified for escort work. The former is armed with four 5-inch D.P. (2 × 2), four 3-inch A.A. (2 × 2), two 20 mm. A.A. (2 × 1) guns, and one 12-inch A/S mortar: and the latter with four 3-inch A.A. (2 × 2), three 20 mm. A.A. (3 × 1) guns, two 12-inch A/S (2 × 1) mortars, and one Hedgehog ATW.

B

Hull No.	Name	Builder	Launched	Fate
DD.837	*Sarsfield*	Bath I.W.	27.5.45	EDD.837 (1959).
DD.838	*Ernest G. Small*	,,	14.6.45	DDR.838 (1952), mined off Hungnam 7/10/51 and repaired with bow of uncompleted *Seymour D. Owen* (DD.767), DD.838 (1969).
DD.839	*Power*	,,	30.6.45	
DD.840	*Glennon (ii)*	,,	14.7.45	
DD.841	*Noa (ii)*	,,	30.7.45	
DD.842	*Fiske (ii)*	,,	8.9.45	DDR.842 (1952), DD.842 (1963).
DD.843	*Warrington (ii)*	,,	27.9.45	
DD.844	*Perry (ii)*	,,	25.10.45	
DD.845	*Baussell*	,,	19.11.45	
DD.846	*Ozbourn*	,,	22.12.45	

Hull No.	Name	Builder	Launched	Fate
DD.847	*Robert L. Wilson*	Bath I.W.	5.1.46	DDE.847 (1950), DD.847 (1962).
DD.848	*Witek*	,,	2.2.46	EDD.848 (1949), DDE.848 (1950); stricken 17/9/68 and expended for experimental purposes.
DD.849	*Richard E. Kraus*	,,	2.3.46	EDD.849 (1949), AG.51 (1952), DD.849 (1954).
DD.850	*Joseph P. Kennedy Jr.*	Bethlehem (Quincy)	26.7.45	
DD.851	*Rupertus*	,,	21.9.45	
DD.852	*Leonard F. Mason*	,,	4.1.46	
DD.853	*Charles H. Roan* (ii)	,,	15.3.46	
DD.854	Unnamed	Bethlehem (Staten Island)	—	Cancelled 12/8/45.
DD.855	Unnamed	,,	—	Cancelled 12/8/45.
DD.856	Unnamed	,,	—	Cancelled 12/8/45

Hull No.	Name	Builder	Launched	Fate
DD.858	Fred T. Berry	Bethlehem (San Pedro)	28.1.45	DDK.858 (1949), DDE.858 (1950) DDK.858 (1962), stricken 15/9/70 and scrapped.
DD.859	Norris	,,	25.2.45	DDK.859 (1949), DDE.859 (1950), DD.859 (1962).
DD.860	McCaffery	,,	12.4.45	DDK.860 (1949), DDE.860 (1950), DD.860 (1962).
DD.861	Harwood	,,	24.5.45	DDK.861 (1949), DDE.861 (1950), DD.861 (1962).
DD.862	Vogelgesang (ii)	Bethlehem (Staten Island)	15.1.45	
DD.863	Steinaker (ii)	,,	13.2.45	DDR.863 (1949), DD.863 (1963).
DD.864	Harold J. Ellison (ii)	,,	14.3.45	
DD.865	Charles R. Ware (ii)	,,	12.4.45	
DD.866	Cone	,,	10.5.45	
DD.867	Stribling	,,	8.6.45	

The TIMMERMAN (*above*) and the GLENNON (*right*) were both completed post-war and omitted all T.T. for enhanced A.A. defence

The TIMMERMAN was fitted with special experimental machinery using high pressure steam.

Hull No.	Name	Builder	Launched	Fate
DD.868	*Brownson (ii)*	Bethlehem (Staten Island)	7.7.45	
DD.869	*Arnold J. Isbell*	,,	6.8.45	
DD.870	*Fechteler (ii)*	,,	19.9.45	DDR.870 (1953), DD.870 (1963); stricken 11/9/70 and scrapped.
DD.871	*Damato*	,,	21.11.45	DDE.871 (1950), DD.871 (1962).
DD.872	*Forrest Royal*	,,	17.1.46	
DD.873	*Hawkins (ex-Beatty)*	Consolidated Steel Corp. (Orange)	7.10.44	DDR.873 (1949), DD.873 (1963).
DD.874	*Duncan (ii)*	,,	27.10.44	DDR.874 (1949), DD.874 (1969).
DD.875	*Henry W. Tucker (ii)*	,,	8.11.44	DDR.875 (1949), DD.875 (1963).
DD.876	*Rogers*	,,	20.11.44	DDR.876 (1949), DD.876 (1963).
DD.877	*Perkins (ii)*	,,	7.12.44	DDR.877 (1949), DD.877 (1962).

The GYATT *re-armed with twin Terrier launch arms aft as the first guided missile destroyer (DDG) in the U.S. Navy. Twin 3inch A.A. mountings are fitted amidships and a Hedgehog ATW abaft "B" turret, while a tripod foremast carried tracking and guidance RDF.*

Hull No.	Name	Builder	Launched	Fate
DD.878	*Vesole*	Consolidated Steel Corp. (Orange)	29.12.44	DDR.878 (1949), DD.878 (1963).
DD.879	*Leary (ii)*	,,	20.1.45	DDR.879 (1949), DD.879 (1963).
DD.880	*Dyess*	,,	26.1.45	DDR.880 (1949), DD.880 (1963).
DD.881	*Bordelon*	,,	3.3.45	DDR.881 (1949), DD.881 (1962).
DD.882	*Furse*	,,	9.3.45	DDR.882 (1949), DD.882 (1962).
DD.883	*Newman K. Perry*	,,	17.3.45	DDR.883 (1949), DD.883 (1962).
DD.884	*Floyd B. Parkes*	,,	31.3.45	Damaged collision cruiser *Columbus* off Luzon 11/3/56 and repaired with bow of uncompleted *Lansdale* (DD.766).
DD.885	*John R. Craig*	,,	14.4.45	
DD.886	*Orleck*	,,	12.5.45	
DD.887	*Brinkley Bass*	,,	26.5.45	

Hull No.	Name	Builder	Launched	Fate
DD.888	*Stickel*	Consolidated Steel Corp. (Orange)	16.6.45	DDR.888 (1949), DD.888 (1962).
DD.889	*O'Hare*	,,	22.6.45	DDR.889 (1949), DD.889 (1962).
DD.890	*Meredith (iii)*	,,	28.6.45	
DD.891	Unnamed	Federal Sbdg. (Kearny)	—	Cancelled 8/3/45.
DD.892	Unnamed	,,	—	Cancelled 8/3/45.
DD.893	Unnamed	,,	—	Cancelled 8/3/45.
DD.894	Unnamed	Consolidated Steel Corp. (Orange)	—	Cancelled 27/3/45.
DD.895	Unnamed	,,	—	Cancelled 27/3/45.
DD.896 to DD.904	Unnamed	Bath I.W.	—	Cancelled 28/3/45.
DD.905 to DD.908	Unnamed	Boston N.Y.	—	Cancelled 27/3/45.

Hull No.	Name	Builder	Launched	Fate
DD.909 to DD.916	Unnamed	Bethlehem (Staten Island)	—	Cancelled 28/3/45.
DD.917 to DD.924	Unnamed	Consolidated Steel Corp. (Orange)	—	Cancelled 27/3/45.
DD.925	Unnamed	Charleston N.Y.	—	Cancelled 27/3/45.
DD.926	Unnamed	,,	—	Cancelled 27/3/45.
DD.927	Unnamed	Bath I.W.	—	Completed as DL.2.
DD.928	Unnamed	,,	—	Completed as DL.3.
DD.929	Unnamed	Bethlehem (Quincy)	—	Completed as DL.4.
DD.930	Unnamed	,,	—	Completed as DL.5.

Machinery contracts: *DD.710–712, 714, 715, 717, 718, 742, 743, 822, 823, 850–853, 859, 868–870, 879, 880* and *886* engined by Westinghouse; *DD.764, 765* and *789* by Allis-Chalmers; and all others—except cancelled *DD.809–816, 854–856* and *891–930*—by General Electric.

With the division of ex-enemy warships among the Allied navies at the close of the European and Pacific wars the following destroyers and destroyer escorts were allocated to the United States Navy:-

ex-German: **T.4, T.14, T.19, T.21, T.35, Z.29, Z.34, Z.39.**

ex-Japanese **HANATSUKI, KABA, KAKI, KASHK, KEYAKI, ODAKAZE.**

of which only the *Hanatsuki*, *T.35*, and *Z.39* were formally commissioned as American warships for brief experimental periods.

Hull No.	Name	Builder	Launched	Fate
DD.934	Unnamed (ex-I.J.N. *Hanatsuki*)	Maizuru	10.10.44	Expended as target . . . . /. ./48.
DD.935	Unnamed (ex-German *T.35*)	Schichau (Elbing)	44	French Navy (1947) and cannibalised for spares.
DD.939	Unnamed (ex-German *Z.39*)	Germania Werft (Kiel)	2.12.41	French Navy (1948) and cannibalised for spares.

Machinery contracts: All engined by builders.

Below: *The ex-German destroyer Z.39*

"Evarts" class: **ANDRES, AUSTIN, BEBAS, BRACKET, BRENNAN, BURDEN R. HASTINGS, CABANA, CANFIELD, CARLSON, CHARLES R. GREER, CLOUES, CONNOLLY, CREAMER, CROUTER, CROWLEY, DECKER, DEEDE, DELBERT W. HALSEY, DEMPSEY, DIONNE, DOBLER, DOHERTY, DONALDSON, DONEFF, DUFFY, EDGAR G. CHASE, EDWARD C. DALY, EISELE, ELDEN, ELY, EMERY, ENGSTROM, EVARTS, FAIR, FINNEGAN, FLEMING, GILMORE, GREINER, GRISWOLD, HALLORAN, HAROLD G. THOMAS, JOHN J. POWERS, JOHN M. BERMINGHAM, KEPPLER, LAKE, LEHARDY, LLOYD THOMAS, LOVERING, LYMAN, MANLOVE, MARTIN, MASON, MITCHELL, O'TOOLE, RALL, REYNOLDS, SANDERS, SEDERSTROM, SEID, SMART, STADFELD, STEELE, TISDALE, WALTER S. BROWN, WHITMAN, WILEMAN, WILLARD KEITH, WILLIAM C. LAWES, WILLIAM C. MILLER, WINTLE, WYFFELS, WYMAN, ONE** unnamed vessel, and **THIRTY-TWO** units for the Royal Navy.

Under the terms of the "Lend/Lease" agreement, the destroyer escort was designed to meet a pressing British requirement for escort vessels (they were classed as frigates by the Royal Navy) and an initial order for fifty was placed early in 1941. While the design was cast to meet a basic British concept—a length of 300 feet for ocean work, a speed of 20 knots, and a large radius of action—it was wholly American in planning and execution.

As the only machinery available for quantity production was a diesel engine in the medium power range it meant a multi-unit arrangement for each shaft, and therefore diesel-electric propulsion was chosen as the less desirable alternative was a direct diesel drive which entailed a complicated gear train. As a result of higher priorities in other categories the diesel engines were in short supply, and so as not to arrest production the designed power was halved. Consequently, speed was reduced to 21 knots with 6,000 B.H.P., instead of the intended 24 knots with 12,000 S.H.P., but this was still adequate for escort duties.

Following contemporary destroyer construction they had a flush-decked hull, were rigged with a pole foremast, and were armed for escort work with A.A. and A/S weapons. While slower than the British escort destroyers they were better armed and equipped than the British frigates, and although the Royal Navy viewed their tophamper with a certain degree of reserve they nonetheless weathered the severe conditions experienced in the North Atlantic.

The BURDEN HASTINGS *showing detached superstructure block applicable to only "short-hulled" destroyer escorts.*

Displacement:	1,140 tons (1,360 tons full load).
Dimensions:	283½(wl) 289½(oa) × 35 × 8¼ (11 full load) feet.
Machinery:	Two shafts; General Motors diesel engines and electric motors B.H.P. 6,000 = 21 knots.
Bunkers and radius:	O.F. 126 tons; 5,000 miles at 15 knots.
Armament:	Three 3-inch/50 cal. D.P. (3 × 1), four 1·1-inch/75 cal. A.A. (1 × 4—in *DE.5–11, 19–44, 47–50, 256–265, 301–315* and *527–530*) or two 40 mm. A.A. (1 × 2—in *DE.13–18* and *45*), nine 20 mm. A.A. (9 × 1) guns; one A/S spigot mortar (Hedgehog), eight A/S mortars and two racks for DC's.
Complement:	156 (war 198).

Hull No.	Name	Builder	Launched	Fate
DE.1	Unnamed	Boston N.Y.	27.6.42	R.N. *Bayntun* (1943); returned U.S.N. 22/8/45 and scrapped.
DE.2	Unnamed	,,	27.6.42	R.N. *Bazely* (1943); returned U.S.N. 20/8/45 and scrapped.
DE.3	Unnamed	,,	23.11.42	R.N. *Berry* (*ii*) (1943); returned U.S.N. 15/2/46 and scrapped.
DE.4	Unnamed	,,	23.11.42	R.N. *Blackwood* (*ii*) (1943); torpedoed German submarine *U.764* south of Portland 15.6.42.
DE.5	*Evarts*	,,	7.12.42	Sold .... 12/7/46 and scrapped.
DE.6	*Wyffels*	,,	7.12.42	Chinese Navy (Nationalist) *Tai Kang* (1945).
DE.7	*Griswold*	,,	9.1.43	Sold ..../12/46 and scrapped.
DE.8	*Steele*	,,	9.1.43	Sold ..../12/46 and scrapped.

The armament arrangement as shown in WYMAN *(above) was standard **for all 3-inch-gunned** destroyer escorts.*

Hull No.	Name	Builder	Launched	Fate
DE.9	*Carlson*	Boston N.Y.	9.1.43	Sold .... 17/12/46 and scrapped.
DE.10	*Bebas*	,,	9.1.43	Sold .... 8/1/47 and scrapped.
DE.11	*Crouter*	,,	26.1.43	Sold .... 25/11/46 and scrapped.
DE.12	Unnamed	,,	26.1.43	R.N. *Burges* (*ii*) (1943); returned U.S.N. 27/2/46 and scrapped.
DE.13	*Brennan* (ex-R.N. *Bentinck*)	Mare Island N.Y. (Vallejo)	22.8.42	Sold .... 12/7/46 and scrapped.
DE.14	*Doherty* (ex-R.N. *Berry*)	,,	29.8.42	Sold .... 26/12/46 and scrapped.
DE.15	*Austin* (ex-R.N. *Blackwood*)	,,	25.9.42	Sold ..../1/47 and scrapped.
DE.16	*Edgar G. Chase* (ex-R.N. *Burges*)	,,	26.9.42	Sold .... 18/3/47 and scrapped.

Hull No.	Name	Builder	Launched	Fate
DE.17	Edward C. Daly (ex-R.N. Byard)	Mare Island N.Y. (Vallejo)	21.10.42 22.10.42	Sold .... 8/1/47 and scrapped.
DE.18	Gilmore (ex-R.N. Calder)	,,	22.10.42	Sold ..../2/47 and scrapped.
DE.19	Burden R. Hastings (ex-R.N. Duckworth)	,,	20.11.42	Sold .... 1/2/47 and scrapped.
DE.20	LeHardy (ex-R.N. Duff)	,,	21.11.42	Sold National Metal and Steel Corp. (Terminal Island) 26/12/46 and scrapped.
DE.21	Harold C. Thomas (ex-R.N. Essington)	,,	18.12.42	Sold ..../1/47 and scrapped.
DE.22	Wileman (ex-R.N. Foley)	,,	19.12.42	Sold ..../1/47 and scrapped.
DE.23	Charles R. Greer	,,	18.1.43	Sold .... 1/2/47 and scrapped.
DE.24	Whitman	,,	19.1.43	Sold ..../1/47 and scrapped.

C

Hull No.	Name	Builder	Launched	Fate
DE.25	Wintle (ii)	Mare Island N.Y. (Vallejo)	18.2.43	Sold . . . ./7/47 and scrapped.
DE.26	Dempsey (ii)	,,	19.2.43	Sold . . . . 18/4/47 and scrapped.
DE.27	Duffy (ii)	,,	16.4.43	Sold . . . . 16/6/47 and scrapped.
DE.28	Emery (ex-Eisner)	,,	17.4.43	Sold . . . . 21/7/47 and scrapped.
DE.29	Stadtfeld	,,	17.5.43	Sold . . . ./7/47 and scrapped.
DE.30	Martin	,,	18.5.43	Sold Wilmington Transportation Co. (Wilmington) 15/5/47 and scrapped.
DE.31	Sederstrom (ex-Gillette)	,,	15.6.43	Sold . . . ./1/48 and scrapped.
DE.32	Fleming (ii)	,,	16.6.43	Sold . . . . 29/1/48 and scrapped.

Hull No.	Name	Builder	Launched	Fate
DE.33	Tisdale (ii)	Mare Island N.Y. (Vallejo)	28.6.43	Sold ..../2/48 and scrapped.
DE.34	Eisele (ii)	,,	29.6.43	Sold .... 29/1/48 and scrapped.
DE.35	Fair	,,	27.7.43	U.S. Army (1947).
DE.36	Manlove	,,	28.7.43	Sold A. G. Schoonmaker Co. Inc. (New York) 4/12/47 and scrapped.
DE.37	Greiner	Puget Sound N.Y. (Bremerton)	20.5.43	Sold ..../2/47 and scrapped.
DE.38	Wyman	,,	3.6.43	Sold ..../5/47 and scrapped.
DE.39	Lovering (ii)	,,	18.6.43	Sold Hugo New Inc. (New York) 31/12/46 and scrapped.
DE.40	Sanders (ii)	,,	18.6.43	Sold ..../5/47 and scrapped.

Hull No.	Name	Builder	Launched	Fate
DE.41	*Brackett*	Puget Sound N.Y. (Bremerton)	1.8.43	Sold .... 22/5/47 and scrapped.
DE.42	*Reynolds*	,,	1.8.43	Sold ..../4/47 and scrapped.
DE.43	*Mitchell*	,,	1.8.43	Sold Puget Sound Navigation Co., (Seattle) 11/12/46 and scrapped, machinery installed in mercantile *Evergreen State* (1954).
DE.44	*Donaldson (ii)*	,,	1.8.43	Sold .... 2/7/46 and scrapped.
DE.45	*Andres* (ex-R.N. *Capel*)	Philadelphia N.Y.	24.7.42	Sold ..../1/46 and scrapped.
DE.46	Unnamed	,,	24.7.42	R.N. *Cockburn* (1943), *Drury* (1943); returned U.S.N. 20/8/45 and scrapped.
DE.47	*Decker*	,,	24.7.42	Chinese Navy (Nationalist) *Tai Ping* (1945); torpedoed Chinese Navy (Communist) MTB off Tachen Islands 14/11/54.
DE.48	*Dobler*	,,	24.7.42	Sold .... 12/7/46 and scrapped.

Hull No.	Name	Builder	Launched	Fate
DE.49	*Doneff*	Philadelphia N.Y.	24.7.42	Sold .... 9/1/47 and scrapped.
DE.50	*Engstrom*	,,	24.7.42	Sold .... 26/12/46 and scrapped.
DE.256	*Seid*	Boston N.Y.	22.2.43	Sold ..../1/47 and scrapped.
DE.257	*Smart*	,,	22.2.43	Sold ..../7/46 and scrapped.
DE.258	*Walter S. Brown*	,,	22.2.43	Sold ..../7/46 and scrapped.
DE.259	*William C. Miller*	,,	22.2.43	Sold ..../4/47 and scrapped.
DE.260	*Cabana*	,,	10.3.43	Sold .... 13/5/47 and scrapped.
DE.261	*Dionne*	,,	10.3.43	Sold .... 12/6/47 and scrapped.

Hull No.	Name	Builder	Launched	Fate
DE.262	*Canfield*	Boston N.Y.	6.4.43	Sold .... 12/6/47 and scrapped.
DE.263	*Deede*	,,	6.4.43	Sold .... 12/6/47 and scrapped.
DE.264	*Elden*	,,	6.4.43	Sold .... 12/7/47 and scrapped.
DE.265	*Cloues*	,,	6.4.43	Sold .... 22/5/47 and scrapped.
DE.266	*Wintle* (*i*)	,,	22.4.43	R.N. *Capel* (1943); torpedoed German submarine *U.486* off Cherbourg 26/12/44.
DE.267	*Dempsey* (*i*)	,,	22.4.43	R.N. *Cooke* (1943); returned U.S.N. 5/3/46 and scrapped.
DE.268	*Duffy* (*i*)	,,	14.5.43	R.N. *Dacres* (1943); returned U.S.N. 26/1/46 and scrapped.
DE.269	*Eisner* (*i*)	,,	14.5.43	R.N. *Domett* (1943); returned U.S.N. 5/3/46 and scrapped.

Hull No.	Name	Builder	Launched	Fate
DE.270	Gillette (i)	Boston N.Y.	19.5.43	R.N. Foley (1943); returned U.S.N. 22/8/45 and scrapped.
DE.271	Fleming (i)	,,	19.5.43	R.N. Garlies (1943); returned U.S.N. 20/8/45, sold Thomas A. Barker (........) 18/7/47, and scrapped.
DE.272	Lovering (i)	,,	4.6.43	R.N. Gould (1943); torpedoed German submarine U.358 North Atlantic 1/3/44.
DE.273	Sanders (i)	,,	4.6.43	R.N. Grindall (1943); returned U.S.N. 20/8/45 and arrived Philadelphia N.Y. 28/5/46 for scrapping.
DE.274	O'Toole (i)	,,	8.7.43	R.N. Gardiner (1943); returned U.S.N. 12/2/46 and scrapped.
DE.275	Reybold (i)	,,	8.7.43	R.N. Goodall (1943); torpedoed German submarine U.968 off Kola Inlet 29/4/45.
DE.276	George (i)	,,	8.7.43	R.N. Goodson (1943); torpedoed German submarine U.964 English Channel 25/6/44 and written-off as constructive total loss, sold John Lee (Belfast) 9/1/47 and scrapped.
DE.277	Herzog (i)	,,	8.7.43	R.N. Gore (1943); returned U.S.N. 2/5/46 and scrapped.

Hull No.	Name	Builder	Launched	Fate
DE.278	*Tisdale* (i)	Boston N.Y.	17.7.43	R.N. *Keats* (1943); returned U.S.N. 27/2/46 and scrapped.
DE.279	*Trumpeter* (i)	,,	17.7.43	R.N. *Kempthorne* (1943); returned U.S.N. 20/8/45 and scrapped.
DE.280	Unnamed	,,	13.8.43	R.N. *Kingsmill* (1943); returned U.S.N. 22/8/45 and scrapped.
DE.301	*Lake*	Mare Island N.Y. (Vallejo)	18.8.43	Sold Puget Sound Navigation Co. (Seattle) 14/12/46 and scrapped.
DE.302	*Lyman*	,,	19.8.43	Sold Puget Sound Navigation Co., (Seattle) 26/12/46 and scrapped.
DE.303	*Crowley*	,,	22.9.43	Sold .... 21/12/46 and scrapped.
DE.304	*Rall*	,,	23.9.43	Sold ..../3/47 and scrapped.
DE.305	*Halloran*	,,	14.1.44	Sold ..../3/47 and scrapped.

Hull No.	Name	Builder	Launched	Fate
DE.306	*Connolly*	Mare Island N.Y. (Vallejo)	15.1.44	Sold .... 20/5/46 and scrapped.
DE.307	*Finnegan* (ex-R.N. *Calder*)	,,	22.2.44	Sold ..../5/46 and scrapped.
DE.308	*Creamer*	,,	23.2.44	Cancelled 5/9/44 and scrapped.
DE.309	*Ely*	,,	10.4.44	Cancelled 5/9/44 and scrapped.
DE.310	*Delbert W. Halsey*	,,	11.4.44	Cancelled 5/9/44 and scrapped.
DE.311	*Keppler* (*i*)	,,	—	Cancelled 13/3/44 and scrapped on slip.
DE.312	*Lloyd Thomas* (*i*)	,,	—	Cancelled 13/3/44 and scrapped on slip.
DE.313	*William C. Lawe* (*i*)	,,	—	Cancelled 13/3/44 and scrapped on slip.
DE.314	*Willard Keith* (*i*)	,,	—	Cancelled 13/3/44 and scrapped on slip.
DE.315	Unnamed	,,	—	Cancelled 13/3/44 and scrapped on slip.

Hull No.	Name	Builder	Launched	Fate
DE.516	Unnamed	Boston N.Y.	13.8.43	R.N. *Lawford* (1943); bombed German aircraft off Normandy 8/6/44.
DE.517	Unnamed	,,	13.8.43	R.N. *Louis* (1943); returned U.S.N. 20/3/46, sold State of Pennsylvania 17/6/46, and scrapped.
DE.518	Unnamed	,,	13.8.43	R.N. *Lawson* (1943); returned U.S.N. 20/3/46 and scrapped.
DE.519	Unnamed	,,	30.8.43	R.N. *Lindsay* (1943), *Pasley* (1943); returned U.S.N. 20/8/45 and scrapped.
DE.520	Unnamed	,,	30.8.43	R.N. *Loring* (1943); returned U.S.N. 7/1/47 and scrapped.
DE.521	Unnamed	,,	24.9.43	R.N. *Mitchell* (1943), *Hoste* (1943); returned U.S.N. 22/8/45 and arrived Philadelphia N.Y. 7/5/46 for scrapping.
DE.522	Unnamed	,,	24.9.43	R.N. *Moorsom* (1943); returned U.S.N. 25/10/45 and scrapped.
DE.523	Unnamed	,,	24.9.43	R.N. *Manners* (1943); torpedoed German submarine *U.1172* enroute Falmouth/Liverpool 26/1/45 and written-off as constructive total loss, sold Athens Piraeus Electricity Co. (Athens) 3/12/46 and scrapped.

Hull No.	Name	Builder	Launched	Fate
DE.524	Unnamed	Boston N.Y.	24.9.43	R.N. *Mounsey* (1943); returned U.S.N. 27/2/46, sold North American Smelting Co. (Philadelphia) 8/11/46 and scrapped.
DE.525	Unnamed	,,	2.11.43	R.N. *Inglis* (1944); returned U.S.N. 20/3/46, sold C. B. Boldridge (Bay, Ohio) ../9/47 and scrapped.
DE.526	Unnamed	,,	2.11.43	R.N. *Inman* (1944) returned U.S.N. 1/3/46, sold G. H. Nutman Inc., (Brooklyn) ../11/46, and scrapped.
DE.527	*O'Toole (ii)*	,,	2.11.43	Sold ..../2/46 and scrapped.
DE.528	*John J. Powers*	,,	2.11.43	Sold ..../1/46 and scrapped.
DE.529	*Mason*	,,	17.11.43	Sold ..../3/47 and scrapped.
DE.530	*John M. Bermingham*	,,	17.11.43	Sold Thomas Harris Harris (Barber, N.J.) ../2/46 and scrapped.

Machinery contracts: All engined by General Motors.

"Buckley" class: **AHRENS, ALEXANDER J. LUKE, AMESBURY, BARBER, BARR, BATES, BLESSMAN, BORUM, BOWERS, BUCKLEY, BULL, BUNCH, BURKE, CHARLES LAWRENCE, CHASE, COFER, COOLBAUGH, CRONIN, CURRIER, DAMON M. CUMMINGS, DANIEL T. GRIFFIN, DARBY, DONNELL, DURIK, EARL V. JOHNSON, EICHENBERGER, ENGLAND, ENRIGHT, FECHTELER, FIEBERLING, FOGG, FOREMAN, FOSS, FOWLER, FRAMENT, FRANCIS M. ROBINSON, FRYBARGER, GANTNER, GENDREAU, GILLETTE, GEORGE, GEORGE W. INGRAM, GREENWOOD, GUNASON, HAINES, HARMON, HAYTER, HENRY R. KENYON, HOLLIS, HOLTON, HOPPING, IRA JEFFERY, J. DOUGLAS BLACKWOOD, JACK C. WILKE, JAMES E. CRAIG, JENKS, JOSEPH C. HUBBARD, JOSEPH E. CAMPBELL, JORDAN, KEPHART, LANING, LEE FOX, LIDDLE, LLOYD, LOESER, LOVELACE, LOY, MAJOR, MALOY, MANNING, MARSH, NEUENDORF, NEWMAN, OSMUS, OTTER, PAUL G. BAKER, RABY, REEVES, RICH, ROBERT I. PAINE, RUEBEN JAMES, RUNELS, SCHMITT, SCOTT, SCROGGINS, SIMS, SOLAR, SPANGENBERG, SPANGLER, TATUM, THOMASON, UNDERHILL, VAMMEN, VARIAN, WEBER, WEEDEN, WHITEHURST, WILLIAM C. COLE, WILLIAM T. POWELL, WILLMARTH, WISEMAN, WITTER** and **FORTY-SIX** units for the Royal Navy.

Once the United States was involved in the Second World War they were equally beset by an acute shortage of escort vessels. They were fortunate in having the destroyer escort in production for the Royal Navy and it was promptly incorporated into the United States Navy. A further two hundred were on order by early 1942.

As diesel engines were still in short supply this class was given turbo-electric propulsion so that the full design power requirements could be met. The hull was slightly lengthened to accommodate the steam plant, which adopted the unit arrangement with boiler and engine rooms alternated.

Six units—*Yokes, Pavlic, Odum, Jack C. Robinson, Bassett,* and *John B. Gray*—were completed as fast transports (APD.69–74), and between 1944–45 a further thirty-nine units were similarly converted (APD.37–40, 42–63, 65, 66 and 75–86 while six other scheduled conversions (APD.41, 64, 67, 68, 82 and 83) were not finally put in hand.

These conversions comprised extending the superstructure out to the ship's side for extra accommodation; four LCA's were nested in pairs on each side amidships and were stowed under boom-headed luffing davits; and a derrick was stepped from a short lattice mast aft for handling military loads. They were re-armed with one 5-inch/38 cal. forward and six 40 mm. A.A. guns in twin mountings (one forward and two aft), with a complement of 204, could accommodate 162 troops.

No T.T. were shipped in *Ahrens, Barr, Alexander J. Luke,* and *Robert I. Paine* which mounted four 40 mm. A.A. (4 × 1) guns in lieu, and other units were similarly altered during 1944–45. In 1945 *Coolbaugh, Darby, J. Douglas Dashwood, Harmon, Greenwood, Loeser, Spangler, George, Raby, Currier,* and *Osmus* had their T.T. removed and were re-armed with two 5-inch/38 cal. D.P. (2 × 1) and ten 40 mm. A.A. (1 × 4 and 3 × 2) guns. Similarly re-armed were *Buckley, Fogg, Rueben James, William T. Powell, Spangenberg, Alexander J. Luke,* and *Robert I. Paine* which had a tripod mast stepped abaft the funnel to carry AW.RDF for duty as radar pickets (DER).

Displacement:	1,400 tons (1,720 tons full load).
Dimensions:	300 (wl) 306 (oa) × 37 except *DE.153–161, 198–223, 665–673, 693–705* and *789–800* 36¾ × 9½ (13½ full load) feet.
Machinery:	Two Babcock & Wilcox (in *DE.153, 154, 156–161, 198, 214–223* and *789–800*) or Combustion Engineering (in *DE.155, 199–213, 633–644, 675–683* and *693–705*) or Foster Wheeler (in *DE.51–98, 563–578* and *665–673*) boilers; two shafts; General Electric turbines and electric motors S.H.P. 12,000 = 24 except *DE.51–98, 563–758, 633–644* and *675–683* 23½ knots.
Bunkers and radius:	O.F. 378 tons; 5,500 miles at 15 knots.
Armament:	Three 3-inch/50 cal. D.P. (3 × 1), four 1·1-inch/75 cal. A.A. (1 × 4) except *DE.153* two 40 mm. A.A. (1 × 2), four 40 mm. A.A. (4 × 1) in *DE.575–578* only, eight except *DE.638–644, 704, 705, 799* and *800* ten and *DE.575–578* six 20 mm. A.A. (6/8/10 × 1) guns; three except *DE.575–578* nil 21-inch (1 × 3) T.T.; one A/S spigot mortar (Hedgehog), eight A/S mortars, and two racks for DC's.
Complement:	186 (war 220).

Hull No.	Name	Builder	Launched	Fate
DE.51	*Buckley*	Bethlehem-Hingham	9.1.43	DER.51 (1949); DE.51 (1954); stricken 1/6/68 and scrapped.
DE.52	*Bull (i)*	,,	22.8.42	R.N. *Bentinck (ii)* (1943); returned U.S.N. 5/1/46 and scrapped.
DE.53	*Charles Lawrence*	,,	16.2.43	APD.37 (1944); sold Southern Scrap Material Co., arrived New Orleans 21/2/66 for scrapping.
DE.54	*Daniel T. Griffin*	,,	25.2.43	APD.38 (1944); Chilean Navy *Uribe* (1967).
DE.55	*Donaldson (i)*	,,	6.3.43	R.N. *Byard (ii)* (1943); returned U.S.N. 12/12/45 and scrapped.
DE.56	*Donnell*	,,	13.3.43	Torpedoed German submarine *U.765* north of Iceland 3/5/44, hulked as floating power station (IX.182–1944); sold .... 29/4/46 and scrapped.
DE.57	*Fogg*	,,	20.3.43	DER.57 (1949), DE.57 (1954); sold Portsmouth Salvage Corp. ../1/66 and scrapped.
DE.58	*Formoe (i)*	,,	27.3.43	R.N. *Calder (ii)* (1943); returned U.S.N. 19/10/45 and scrapped.

The DE hull was slightly lengthened to adopt steam machinery in the "Buckley" class, the superstructure was made continuous, and the funnel conspicuously trunked as shown above in DANIEL T. GRIFFIN.

Hull No.	Name	Builder	Launched	Fate
DE.59	*Foss*	Bethlehem-Hingham	10.4.43	Stricken 1/11/65 and scrapped.
DE.60	*Gantner*	,,	17.4.43	APD.42 (1945); Chinese Navy (Nationalist) *Wen Shan* (1966).
DE.61	*Gary*	,,	1.5.43	R.N. *Duckworth* (*ii*) (1943); returned U.S.N. 17/12/45 and scrapped.
DE.62	*George W. Ingram*	,,	8.5.43	APD.43 (1945); Chinese Navy (Nationalist) *Kang Shan* (1967)
DE.63	*Ira Jeffrey*	,,	15.5.43	APD.44 (1945); stricken ../../60 and scrapped.
DE.64	*Lamons* (*i*)	,,	22.5.43	R.N. *Duff* (*ii*) (1943); mined off Netherlands coast 30/11/44 and written-off as constructive total loss, returned U.S.N. 22/8/45 and scrapped.
DE.65	*Lee Fox*	,,	29.5.43	APD.45 (1945); sold Southern Scrap Material Co., arrived New Orleans 21/2/66 for scrapping.
DE.66	*Amesbury*	,,	5.6.43	APD.46 (1945); stricken ../../60 and scrapped.

The Sims *showing 3-inch guns fore and aft with a pedestal director on the bridge: quadruple 1·1-inch A.A. mounting and director at the after end of the superstructure: four 20 mm. A.A. guns before the bridge, four abaft the funnel, and two at the stern: and a triple bank of T.T. amidships. GW.RDF is carried at the masthead with a topmast for the HF/DF aerial.*

D

Hull No.	Name	Builder	Launched	Fate
DE.67	Unnamed	Bethlehem-Hingham	19.6.43	R.N. *Essington* (*ii*) (1943); returned U.S.N. 19/10/45 and scrapped.
DE.68	*Bates*	,,	6.6.43	APD.47 (1944); bombed Japanese aircraft off Okinawa 25/5/45.
DE.69	*Blessman*	,,	19.6.43	APD.48 (1944); Chinese Navy (Nationalist) *Chung Shan* (1967).
DE.70	*Joseph E. Campbell*	,,	26.6.43	APD.49 (1944); Chilean Navy *Riquelme* (1966).
DE.71	*Oswald* (*i*)	,,	30.6.43	R.N. *Affleck* (1943); torpedoed German submarine *U.486* off Cherbourg 26/12/44 and written-off as constructive total loss, mercantile hulk *Nostra Senora de la Luz* (1954).
DE.72	*Harmon* (*i*)	,,	10.7.43	R.N. *Aylmer* (1943); returned U.S.N. 5/11/45 and scrapped.
DE.73	*McAnn* (*i*)	,,	10.7.43	R.N. *Balfour* (1943); returned U.S.N. 25/10/45 and scrapped.
DE.74	*Ebert* (*i*)	,,	17.7.43	R.N. *Bentley* (1943); returned U.S.N. 5/11/45 and scrapped.

A 12-charge pattern could be laid by eight A/S mortars and two racks for eighty deck-stowed DC's as illustrated in GENDRIAN *(above). A clear working area was available for DC crews at the stern, enabling racks and mortars to be rapidly replenished, and the Hedgehog A/S mortar was positioned forward abaft the fo'c'sle gun.*

Hull No.	Name	Builder	Launched	Fate
DE.75	*Eisele* (i)	Bethlehem-Hingham	24.7.43	R.N. *Bickerton* (1943); torpedoed German submarine *U.354* Barents Sea 22/8/44.
DE.76	*Liddle* (i)	,,	31.7.43	R.N. *Bligh* (1943); returned U.S.N. U.S.N. 12/11/45 and scrapped.
DE.77	*Straub* (i)	,,	31.7.43	R.N. *Braithwaite* (1943); returned U.S.N. 13/11/45 and scrapped.
DE.78	Unnamed	,,	7.8.43	R.N. *Bullen* (1943); torpedoed German submarine *U.775* north-west of Scotland 6/12/44.
DE.79	Unnamed	,,	14.8.43	R.N. *Byron* (1943); returned U.S.N. 24/11/45 and scrapped.
DE.80	Unnamed	,,	21.2.43	R.N. *Conn* (1943); returned U.S.N 26/11/45 and scrapped.
DE.81	Unnamed	,,	21.8.43	R.N. *Cotton* (1943); returned U.S.N. 5/11/45 and scrapped.
DE.82	Unnamed	,,	28.8.43	R.N. *Cranstoun* (1943); returned U.S.N. 3/12/45 and scrapped.

Like some other units of the class the CURRIER *had no HF/DF topmast but carried both AW and SW. RDF at the masthead.*

Hull No.	Name	Builder	Launched	Fate
DE.83	Unnamed	Bethlehem-Hingham	11.9.43	R.N. *Cubitt* (1943); returned U.S.N. 4/3/46 and scrapped.
DE.84	Unnamed	,,	18.9.43	R.N. *Curzon* (1943); returned U.S.N. 27/3/46 and scrapped.
DE.85	Unnamed	,,	18.9.43	R.N. *Dakins* (1943); mined off Belgian coast 25/12/44 and written-off as constructive total loss, arrived Netherlands 9/1/47 for scrapping.
DE.86	Unnamed	,,	29.9.43	R.N. *Deane* (1943); returned U.S.N. 4/3/46 and scrapped.
DE.87	Unnamed	,,	2.10.43	R.N. *Ekins* (1943); mined North Sea 16/4/45 and written-off as constructive total loss, arrived Netherlands ../../47 for scrapping.
DE.88	Unnamed	,,	1.9.43	R.N. *Fitzroy* (1943); returned U.S.N. 5/1/46 and scrapped.
DE.89	Unnamed	,,	2.10.43	R.N. *Redmill* (1943); torpedoed German submarine *U.1105* off west coast of Ireland 27/4/45 and written-off as constructive total loss, returned U.S.N. 20/1/47 and scrapped.
DE.90	Unnamed	,,	9.10.43	R.N. *Retalick* (1943); returned U.S.N. 25/10/45 and scrapped.

In the ROBERT I. PAINE *the T.T. have been replaced by four single 40 mm. A.A. guns, and a light tripod mainmast stepped for the HF/DF aerials. A quadruple 1·1-inch A.A. mounting was still shipped aft.*

Hull No.	Name	Builder	Launched	Fate
DE.91	Unnamed	Bethlehem-Hingham	14.10.43	R.N. *Reynolds* (1943), *Halsted* (1943); torpedoed German torpedo boats *Jaguar* and *Moewe* English Channel 11/6/44 and written-off as constructive total loss, cannibalised for spares, arrived Netherlands 28/3/47 for scrapping.
DE.92	Unnamed	,,	23.10.43	R.N. *Riou* (1943); returned U.S.N. 25/2/46 and scrapped
DE.93	Unnamed	,,	23.10.43	R.N. *Rutherford* (1943); returned U.S.N. 25/10/45 and scrapped.
DE.94	Unnamed	,,	30.10.43	R.N. *Reeves* (1943), *Cosby* (1943); returned U.S.N. 4/3/46 and scrapped.
DE.95	Unnamed	,,	30.10.43	R.N. *Rowley* (1943); returned U.S.N. 12/11/45 and scrapped.
DE.96	Unnamed	,,	31.10.43	R.N. *Rupert* (1943); returned U.S.N. 20/3/46 and scrapped.
DE.97	Unnamed	,,	31.10.43	R.N. *Stockham* (1943); returned U.S.N. 15/2/46 and scrapped.
DE.98	Unnamed	,,	1.11.43	R.N. *Seymour* (1943); returned U.S.N. 5/1/46 and scrapped.

The GILLETTE also mounted four additional 40 mm. guns in lieu of the T.T. but has twin 40 mm. in place of the 1·1-inch A.A. mounting aft.

Hull No.	Name	Builder	Launched	Fate
DE.153	Rueben James (ii)	Norfolk N.Y. (Portsmouth)	6.2.43	DER.153 (1949), DE.153 (1954); stricken 30/6/68 and scrapped.
DE.154	Sims (ii)	,,	6.2.43	APD.50 (1944); stricken ../../60 and scrapped.
DE.155	Hopping	,,	10.3.43	APD.51 (1944); sold Boston Metal Corp. (Baltimore) 15/8/66 and scrapped.
DE.156	Reeves	,,	22.4.43	APD.52 (1944); stricken ../../60 and scrapped.
DE.157	Fechteler (i)	,,	22.4.43	Torpedoed German submarine U.967 north-west of Oran 5/5/44.
DE.158	Chase	,,	24.4.43	APD.54 (1944); sold .... 13/11/46 and scrapped.
DE.159	Laning	,,	4.7.43	APD.55 (1944); LPR.55 (1969).
DE.160	Loy	,,	4.7.43	APD.56 (1944); sold Boston Metal Corp. (Baltimore) 15/8/66 and scrapped.

The HARMON *was later re-armed with 5-inch D.P. guns, and a twin 40 mm. A.A. mounting and the Hedgehog A/S mortar replaced the former 3-inch and 20 mm. guns on the superstructure deck forward of the bridge, while two twin 40 mm. and two single 20mm. A.A. replaced the T.T. amidships and a quadruple 40 mm. the original twin mounting at the after end of the superstructure deck.*

Hull No.	Name	Builder	Launched	Fate
DE.161	*Barber*	Norfolk N.Y. (Portsmouth)	20.5.43	APD.57 (1944), LPR.57 (1969).
DE.198	*Lovelace*	,,	4.7.43	Stricken 1/7/67 and expended as target.
DE.199	*Manning*	Charleston N.Y.	1.6.43	Stricken 31/7/68 and scrapped.
DE.200	*Neuendorf*	,,	18.6.43	Stricken 1/7/67 and expended as target.
DE.201	*James E. Craig*	,,	22.7.43	Stricken 30/6/68 and scrapped.
DE.202	*Eichenberger*	,,	22.7.43	
DE.203	*Thomason*	,,	23.8.43	Stricken 30/6/68 and scrapped.
DE.204	*Jordan*	,,	23.8.43	Sold ..../7/47 and scrapped.

Hull No.	Name	Builder	Launched	Fate
DE.205	Newman	Charleston N.Y.	9.8.43	APD.59 (1944); sold Boston Metal Corp. (Baltimore) 15/8/66 and scrapped.
DE.206	Liddle (ii)	,,	9.8.43	APD.60 (1944); sold North American Smelting Co. (Wilmington) 25/1/68 and scrapped.
DE.207	Kephart	,,	6.9.43	APD.61 (1944); South Korean Navy Kyong Buk (1967).
DE.208	Cofer	,,	6.9.43	APD.62 (1944); sold Southern Scrap Materials Co., arrived New Orleans 3/4/68 for scrapping.
DE.209	Lloyd	,,	23.10.43	APD.63 (1944); sold Southern Scrap Materials Co., arrived New Orleans 3/4/68 for scrapping.
DE.210	Otter	,,	23.10.43	Stricken 1/11/69 and scrapped.
DE.211	Joseph C. Hubbard	,,	11.11.43	APD.53 (1945); sold North American Smelting Co. (Wilmington) 1/7/68 and scrapped.
DE.212	Hayter	,,	11.11.43	APD.80 (1945); South Korean Navy Chun Nam (1968).

Hull No.	Name	Builder	Launched	Fate
DE.213	William T. Powell	Charleston N.Y.	27.11.43	DER.213 (1949), DE.213 (1954); sold North American Marine Salvage Corp., arrived Bordertown 25/10/66 for scrapping.
DE.214	Scott	Philadelphia N.Y.	3.4.43	(APD.64); sold Southern Scrap Materials Co., arrived New Orleans 10/2/67 for scrapping.
DE.215	Burke	,,	3.4.43	APD.65 (1945); Colombian Navy *Almirante Brion* (1968)
DE.216	Enright	,,	29.5.43	APD.66 (1945); Ecuadorian Navy *25 de Julio* (1967).
DE.217	Coolbaugh	,,	29.5.43	
DE.218	Darby	,,	29.5.43	Stricken 23/9/68 and scrapped.
DE.219	J. Douglas Blackwood	,,	29.5.43	Stricken 30/1/70 and scrapped.
DE.220	Francis M. Robinson	,,	29.5.43	EDE.220 (1949), DE.220 (1960).

Hull No.	Name	Builder	Launched	Fate
DE.221	*Solar*	Philadelphia N.Y.	29.5.43	Internal explosion . . . . 30/4/46.
DE.222	*Fowler*	,,	3.7.43	Sold Peck Iron & Metal Co., (. . . . .) 29/12/66 and scrapped.
DE.223	*Spangenberg*	,,	3.7.43	DER.223 (1949), DE.223 (1954); sold North American Marine Salvage Co., arrived Bordentown 25/10/66 for scrapping.
DE.563	Unnamed	Bethlehem-Hingham	16.10.43	R.N. *Spragge* (1944); returned U.S.N. 28/2/46 and scrapped.
DE.564	Unnamed	,,	6.11.43	R.N. *Stayner* (1943); returned U.S.N. 24/11/45 and scrapped.
DE.565	Unnamed	,,	13.11.43	R.N. *Thornborough* (1943); returned U.S.N. 29/1/47 and scrapped.
DE.566	Unnamed	,,	20.11.43	R.N. *Trollope* (1944); torpedoed German MTB off Normandy 6/7/44 and written-off as constructive total loss, sold West of Scotland Sbkg. Co. and arrived Troon ../5/51 for scrapping.
DE.567	Unnamed	,,	20.11.43	R.N. *Tyler* (1944); returned U.S.N. 12/11/45 and scrapped.

Hull No.	Name	Builder	Launched	Fate
DE.568	Unnamed	Bethlehem-Hingham	27.11.43	R.N. *Torrington* (1944); returned U.S.N. 11/6/46 and scrapped.
DE.569	Unnamed	,,	27.11.43	R.N. *Narborough* (1944); returned U.S.N. 4/2/46 and scrapped.
DE.570	Unnamed	,,	4.12.43	R.N. *Waldegrave* (1944); returned U.S.N. 3/12/45 and scrapped.
DE.571	Unnamed	,,	12.12.43	R.N. *Whitaker* (1944); torpedoed German submarine *U.483* off Malin Head 1/11/44 and written-off as constructive total loss, returned U.S.N. ../3/45 and scrapped.
DE.572	Unnamed	,,	18.12.43	R.N. *Holmes* (1944); returned U.S.N. 3/12/45, sold Walter H. Wilms & Co. (Detroit) ../10/47 and scrapped
DE.573	Unnamed	,,	18.12.43	R.N. *Hargood* (1944); returned U.S.N. 23/2/46, sold Northern Metal Co. (Tacony, Pa.) 7/3/47 and scrapped.
DE.574	Unnamed	,,	22.12.43	R.N. *Hotham* (1944); returned U.S.N. 13/3/56 and scrapped.
DE.575	*Ahrens*	,,	21.12.43	Sold Southern Scrap Material Co., arrived New Orleans 10/2/67 for scrapping.

Hull No.	Name	Builder	Launched	Fate
DE.576	*Barr*	Bethlehem-Hingham	28.12.43	APD.39 (1944); stricken ../../60 and scrapped.
DE.577	*Alexander J. Luke*	,,	28.12.43	DER.577 (1949), DE.577 (1954); stricken 1/5/70 and scrapped.
DE.578	*Robert I. Paine*	,,	30.12.43	DER.578 (1949), DE.578 (1954); stricken 1/6/68 and scrapped.
DE.633	*Foreman*	Bethlehem (San Francisco)	1.8.43	Sold Boston Metals Corp. (Baltimore) ../../66 and scrapped.
DE.634	*Whitehurst*	,,	5.9.43	Collision mercantile *Hoyanger* off Vancouver 16/1/65; stricken 12/7/69 and scrapped.
DE.635	*England*	,,	26.9.43	Bombed Japanese aircraft off Okinawa 9/5/45 and written-off as constructive total loss, (APD.41); sold .... 26/11/46 and scrapped.
DE.636	*Witter*	,,	17.10.43	APD.58 (1945); stricken ../11/46 and scrapped.
DE.637	*Bowers*	,,	31.10.43	APD.40 (1945), Philippino Navy *Rajah Soliman* (1961); sold Mitsubishi (Japan) 31/1/66 and scrapped.

E

Hull No.	Name	Builder	Launched	Fate
DE.638	Willmarth	Bethlehem (San Francisco)	21.11.43	Sold North American Smelting Co. (Wilmington) 1/7/68 and scrapped.
DE.639	Gendreau	,,	12.12.43	
DE.640	Fieberling	,,	2.4.44	
DE.641	William C. Cole	,,	29.12.43	
DE.642	Paul G. Baker	,,	12.3.44	Sold Nicolai Joffe Corp. (Richmond) ../../70 and scrapped.
DE.643	Damon M. Cummings (ii)	,,	18.4.44	
DE.644	Vammen	,,	21.5.44	Stricken 12/7/69 and scrapped.
DE.665	Jenks	Dravo Corp. (Pittsburg)	11.9.43	(APD.67); sold Southern Scrap Material Co., arrived New Orleans 8/4/68 for scrapping.

Hull No.	Name	Builder	Launched	Fate
DE.666	*Durik*	Dravo Corp. (Pittsburg)	9.10.43	(APD.68); sold Southern Scrap Material Co., arrived New Orleans 22/2/67 for scrapping.
DE.667	*Wiseman*	,,	6.11.43	
DE.668	*Yokes*	Consolidated Steel Corp. (Orange)	27.11.43	APD.69 (1944); stricken 1/4/64 and scrapped.
DE.669	*Pavlic*	,,	18.12.43	APD.70 (1944); sold North American Smelting Co. (Wilmington) 1/7/68 and scrapped.
DE.670	*Odum*	,,	19.1.44	APD.71 (1944); Chilean Navy *Serrano* (1966).
DE.671	*Jack C. Robinson*	,,	8.1.44	APD.72 (1944); Chilean Navy *Orella* (1966).
DE.672	*Bassett*	,,	15.1.44	APD.73 (1944); Colombian Navy *Almirante Tono* (1967).
DE.673	*John B. Gray*	,,	18.3.44	APD.74 (1944); sold Southern Scrap Material Co. (New Orleans) 5/3/68 and scrapped.

Hull No.	Name	Builder	Launched	Fate
DE.675	*Weber*	Bethlehem (Quincy)	1.5.43	APD.75 (1944); stricken ../../60 and scrapped.
DE.676	*Schmitt*	,,	29.5.43	APD.76 (1945); South Korean Navy ·········· (1967).
DE.677	*Frament*	,,	28.6.43	APD.77 (1944); sold-out commercially as floating power station (1961).
DE.678	*Harmon* (ii)	,,	25.7.43	Sold North American Smelting Co. (Wilmington) 30/1/67 and scrapped.
DE.679	*Greenwood*	,,	21.8.43	Sold Lipsett Inc. (Kearny) 6/9/67 and scrapped.
DE.680	*Loeser*	,,	11.9.43	Stricken 23/9/68 and scrapped.
DE.681	*Gillette* (ii)	,,	25.9.43	
DE.682	*Underhill*	,,	15.10.43	Torpedoed (*kaiten*) I.J.N. submarine *I.53* east of Cape Engano 24/7/45.
DE.683	*Henry R. Kenyon*	,,	30.10.43	Sold Nicolas Joffe Corp. (Richmond) ../../70 and scrapped.

Hull No.	Name	Builder	Launched	Fate
DE.693	Bull (ii)	Defoe Sbdg. (Bay City)	25.3.43	APD.78 (1944); Chinese Navy (Nationalist) Lu Shan (1966).
DE.694	Bunch	,,	29.5.43	APD.79 (1944); stricken 1/4/64 and scrapped.
DE.695	Rich (i)	,,	22.6.43	Mined off Normandy 8/6/44.
DE.696	Spangler	,,	15.7.43	
DE.697	George (ii)	,,	14.8.43	Sold Nicolai Joffe Corp. (Richmond) ../../70 and scrapped.
DE.698	Raby	,,	4.9.43	DEC.698 (1950), DE.698 (1957); stricken 1/6/68 and scrapped.
DE.699	Marsh	,,	25.9.43	
DE.700	Currier	,,	14.10.43	Expended as target off San Clemente Island ../7/67.
DE.701	Osmus	,,	4.11.43	

Hull No.	Name	Builder	Launched	Fate
DE.702	*Earl V. Johnson*	Defoe Sbdg. (Bay City)	24.11.43	Sold Southern Scrap Material Co. (New Orleans) 3/9/68 and scrapped.
DE.703	*Holton*	,,	15.12.43	
DE.704	*Cronin (ii)*	,,	5.1.44	DEC.704 (1950), DE.704 (1957); stricken 1/6/70 and scrapped.
DE.705	*Frybarger*	,,	25.1.44	DEC.705 (1950), DE.705 (1957).
DE.789	*Tatum*	Consolidated Steel Corp. (Orange)	7.8.43	APD.81 (1944); stricken ../../60 and scrapped.
DE.790	*Borum*	,,	14.8.43	(APD.82); sold Peck Iron & Metal Co. (............) ../../66 and scrapped.
DE.791	*Maloy*	,,	18.8.43	(APD.83) EDE.791 (1946); sold North American Smelting Co. Wilmington) 11/3/66 scrapped.
DE.792	*Haines*	,,	26.8.43	APD.84 (1944); stricken ../../60 and scrapped.
DE.793	*Runels*	,,	4.9.43	APD.85 (1945); stricken ../../60 and scrapped.

Hull No.	Name	Builder	Launched	Fate
DE.794	*Hollis*	Consolidated Steel Corp (Orange)	11.9.43	APD.86 (1945), LPR.86 (1969).
DE.795	*Gunason*	,,	16.10.43	
DE.796	*Major*	,,	23.10.43	
DE.797	*Weeden*	,,	27.10.43	Stricken 30/6/68 and scrapped.
DE.798	*Varian*	,,	6.11.43	
DE.799	*Scroggins*	,,	6.11.43	Sold Peck Iron & Metal Co. (........) ../../66 and scrapped.
DE.800	*Jack C. Wilke*	,,	18.12.43	EDE.800 (1949), DE.800 (1960).

Machinery contracts: All engined by General Electric.

The WILLIAM T. POWELL *re-armed with 5-inch D.P. guns and rigged with a tripod mast carrying long-range AW.RDF for picket duties.*

"Canon" class: ACREE, AMICK, ATHERTON, BAKER, BANGUST, BARON, BOOTH, BOST-WICK, BREEMAN, BRIGHT, BRONSTEIN, BURROWS, CARROLL, CARTER, CATES, CLARENCE L. EVANS, COFFMAN, COONER, CURTIS W. HOWARD, DAMON CUMMINGS, EARL K. OLSEN, EBERT, EISNER, ELDRIDGE, GANDY, GARFIELD THOMAS, GAYNIER, GEORGE M. CAMPBELL, GUSTAFSON, HEMMINGER, HILBERT, JOHN J. VAN BUREN, KYNE, LAMONS, LEVY, McCLELLAND, McCONNELL, MICKA, MILTON LEWIS, MUIR, NEAL A. SCOTT, O'NEIL, OSTERHAUS, OSWALD, PARKS, RIDDLE, RINEHART, ROBERTS, ROCHE, RUSSELL M. COX, SAMUEL S. MILES, SLATER, SNYDER, STERN, STRAUB, SUTTON, SWEARER, THOMAS, THORNHILL, TILLS, TRUMPETER, WATERMAN, WEAVER, WESSON, WINGFIELD, **THIRTY-SEVEN** unnamed vessels, and **EIGHT** units for the Brazilian Navy and **SIX** units for the French Navy.

With orders now placed for over one thousand destroyer escorts, and turbine manufacturers heavily committed to supply destroyers and above, the problem of the type of propulsion machinery to be installed was generally resolved by fitting what was currently available. Consequently, this class reverted to diesel-electric propulsion, but the longer hull required by the turbine engined ships was made standard regardless of whether this plant, or diesel engines, were installed. Owing to the heavy demands made on diesel engines by tank landing ships (LST) again only half the designed power could be installed.

Displacement:	1,240 tons (1,520 tons full load).
Dimensions:	300(wl) 306(oa) × 36¾ × 8¾ (11¼ full load) feet.
Machinery:	Two shafts; General Motors diesel engines and electric motors B.H.P. 6,000 = 21 knots.
Bunkers and radius:	O.F. 279 tons; 11,500 miles at 11 knots.
Armament:	Three 3-inch/50 cal. D.P. (3 × 1), two 40 mm. A.A. (1 × 2), eight except *DE.740–762* and *765–788* ten 20 mm. A.A. (8/10 × 1) guns; three 21-inch (1 × 3) T.T.; one A/S spigot mortar (Hedgehog), eight A/S mortars and two racks for DC's.
Complement:	186 (war 220).

Hull No.	Name	Builder	Launched	Fate
DE.99	*Canon*	Dravo Corp. (Wilmington)	25.5.43	Brazilian Navy *Baependi* (1944).
DE.100	*Christopher*	,,	19.6.43	Brazilian Navy *Benavente* (1944).
DE.101	*Alger*	,,	8.7.43	Brazilian Navy *Babitonga* (1945); stricken 1964.
DE.102	*Thomas*	,,	31.7.43	Completed Norfolk N.Y. (Portsmouth) Chinese Navy (Nationalist) *Tai Ho* (1948).
DE.103	*Bostwick*	,,	30.8.43	Chinese Navy (Nationalist) *Tai Tsang* (1948).
DE.104	*Breeman*	,,	4.9.43	Completed Norfolk N.Y. (Portsmouth); Chinese Navy (Nationalist) *Tai Hu* (1948).
DE.105	*Burrows*	,,	2.10.43	R.Neth.N. *Van Amstel* (1950); sold Simons Scheepsslooperij (Rotterdam) ../3/68 and scrapped.
DE.106	*Corbesier (i)*	,,	11.11.43	French Navy *Senegalais* (1944), *Yser* (1962); sold Walter Ritscher, arrived Hamburg 18/10/65 for scrapping.

Hull No.	Name	Builder	Launched	Fate
DE.107	*Cronin* (i)	Dravo Corp (Wilmington)	27.11.43	French Navy *Algerien* (1944), *Oise* (1962); sold Walter Ritscher, arrived Hamburg 11/11/65 for scrapping.
DE.108	*Crosley* (i)	,,	17.12.43	French Navy *Tunisien* (1944); returned U.S.N. ../../60 and scrapped.
DE.109	Unnamed	,,	1.1.44	French Navy *Marocain* (1944); returned U.S.N. ../../60 and scrapped.
DE.110	Unnamed	,,	22.1.44	French Navy *Hova* (1944) returned U.S.N. ../../60 and scrapped.
DE.111	Unnamed	.,	12.2.44	French Navy *Somali* (1944), *Arago* (1956).
DE.112	*Carter*	,,	29.2.44	Chinese Navy (Nationalist) *Tai Chao* (1948).
DE.113	*Clarence L. Evans*	,,	22.3.44	French Navy *Berbere* (1952): returned U.S.N. ../../60 and scrapped.
DE.114 to DE.128	Unnamed	,,	—	Cancelled 10/2/43.

Hull No.	Name	Builder	Launched	Fate
DE.162	*Levy*	Federal Sbdg. (Newark)	28.3.43	
DE.163	*McConnell*	,,	28.3.43	
DE.164	*Osterhaus*	,,	18.4.43	
DE.165	*Parks*	,,	18.4.43	
DE.166	*Baron*	,,	9.5.43	Uruguayan Navy *Uruguay* (1952).
DE.167	*Acree*	,,	9.5.43	
DE.168	*Amick*	,,	27.5.43	Japanese M.S.D.F. *Asahi* (1955).
DE.169	*Atherton*	,,	27.5.43	Completed Norfolk N.Y. (Portsmouth); Japanese M.S.D.F. *Hatsuhi* (1955).

In AMICK—*and several other units of the class—four single 40 mm. A.A. guns were shipped in lieu of the T.T. amidships, and a light tripod mainmast stepped to carry HF/DF aerials, while AW and SW.RDF was fitted at the foremast head.*

Hull No.	Name	Builder	Launched	Fate
DE.170	*Booth*	Federal Sbdg. (Newark)	21.6.43	Completed Norfolk N.Y. (Portsmouth); Philippino Navy *Datu Kalantiaw* (1968).
DE.171	*Carroll*	,,	21.6.43	Completed Norfolk N.Y. (Portsmouth); stricken 1/8/65 and scrapped.
DE.172	*Cooner*	,,	25.7.43	
DE.173	*Eldridge*	,,	25.7.43	R.H.N. *Leon* (1951).
DE.174	*Marts*	,,	8.8.43	Brazilian Navy *Bocaina* (1945).
DE.175	*Pennewill*	,,	8.8.43	Brazilian Navy *Bertioga* (1944); stricken 1964.
DE.176	*Micka*	,,	22.8.43	Sold Peck Iron & Metals Co. (..........) 15/5/67 and scrapped.
DE.177	*Reybold (ii)*	,,	22.8.43	Brazilian Navy *Bauru* (1944).

A topmast carrying HF/DF was fitted above the AW.RDF in the SAMUEL S. MILES, *and absence of funnel trunking indicated diesel main propulsion.*

Hull No.	Name	Builder	Launched	Fate
DE.178	*Herzog (ii)*	Federal Sbdg. (Newark)	5.9.43	Brazilian Navy *Berberibe* (1946); stricken 1968.
DE.179	*McAnn (ii)*	,,	5.9.43	Brazilian Navy *Bracui* (1944).
DE.180	*Trumpeter (ii)*	,,	19.9.43	
DE.181	*Straub (ii)*	,,	19.9.43	
DE.182	*Gustafson*	,,	3.10.43	R.Neth.N. *Van Ewijck* (1950); sold Belgian sbkrs. ../8/68 and scrapped.
DE.183	*Samuel S. Miles*	,,	3.10.43	French Navy *Arabe* (1950); returned U.S.N. ../../60 and scrapped.
DE.184	*Wesson*	,,	17.10.43	Italian Navy *Andromeda* (1951).
DE.185	*Riddle*	,,	17.10.43	French Navy *Kabyle* (1950); sold ARDEM, arrived Savona ../../65 for scrapping.

Hull No.	Name	Builder	Launched	Fate
DE.186	*Swearer*	Federal Sbdg. (Newark)	31.10.43	French Navy *Bambara* (1950)ld; so ARDEM, arrived Savona ../../65 for scrapping.
DE.187	*Stern*	,,	31.10.43	R.Neth.N. *Van Zijll* (1951); sold Simons Scheepsslooperij (Rotterdam) ../3/68 and scrapped.
DE.188	*O'Neil*	,,	14.11.43	R.Neth.N. *Dubois* (1951); sold Simons Scheepsslooperij (Rotterdam) ../3/68 and scrapped.
DE.189	*Bronstein*	,,	14.11.43	Uruguayan Navy *Artigas* (1952).
DE.190	*Baker* (ex-*Raby*)	,,	28.11.43	French Navy *Malagache* (1952).
DE.191	*Coffman*	,,	28.11.43	
DE.192	*Eisner* (ii)	,,	12.12.43	R.Neth.N. *De Zeeuw* (1951); sold Eckhardt GmbH (Hamburg) ../3/68 and scrapped.
DE.193	*Garfield Thomas* (ex-*William G. Thomas*)	,,	12.12.43	R.H.N. *Panthir* (1951).
DE.194	*Wingfield*	Federal Sbdg. (Kearny)	30.12.43	French Navy *Sakalave* (1950); stricken ../../60 and scrapped.

Hull No.	Name	Builder	Launched	Fate
DE.195	*Thornhill*	Federal Sbdg. (Kearny)	30.12.43	Italian Navy *Aldebaran* (1951).
DE.196	*Rinehart*	,,	9.1.44	R.Neth.N. *De Bitter* (1950); sold Eckhardt GmbH (Hamburg) ../3/68.
DE.197	*Roche*	,,	9.1.44	Expended as target off .... 11/3/46.
DE.739	*Bangust*	Western Pipe (San Pedro)	6.6.43	Peruvian Navy *Castilla* (1952).
DE.740	*Waterman*	,,	20.6.43	Peruvian Navy *Aguirre* (1952).
DE.741	*Weaver*	,,	4.7.43	Peruvian Navy *Rodriguez* (1951).
DE.742	*Hilbert*	,,	18.7.43	
DE.743	*Lamons* (*ii*)	,,	1.8.43	
DE.744	*Kyne*	,,	15.8.43	

Hull No.	Name	Builder	Launched	Fate
DE.745	*Snyder*	Western Pipe (San Pedro)	29.8.43	
DE.746	*Hemminger*	,,	12.9.43	R.Thai.N. *Pin Klao* (1959).
DE.747	*Bright*	,,	26.9.43	French Navy *Touareg* (1950); sold ARDEM, arrived Savona ../../65 for scrapping.
DE.748	*Tills*	,,	3.10.43	
DE.749	*Roberts*	,,	14.11.43	Stricken 23/9/68 and scrapped.
DE.750	*McClelland*	,,	28.11.43	
DE.751	*Gaynier*	,,	30.1.44	Cancelled 1/9/44 and scrapped.
DE.752	*Curtis W. Howard*	,,	.../1/44	Cancelled 1/9/44 and scrapped.
DE.753	*John J. Van Buren*	,,	16.1.44	Cancelled 1/9/44 and scrapped.

Hull No.	Name	Builder	Launched	Fate
DE.754	Unnamed	Western Pipe (San Pedro)	—	Cancelled 2/10/43 and scrapped on slip.
DE.755	Unnamed	,,	—	Cancelled 2/10/43 and scrapped on slip.
DE.756	*Damon M. Cummings* (*i*)	,,	—	Cancelled 2/10/43.
DE.757 to DE.762	Unnamed	,,	—	Cancelled 2/10/43.
DE.763	*Cates*	Tampa Sbdg.	10.10.43	French Navy *Soudanais* (1950); sold ARDEM, arrived Savona ../../65 for scrapping.
DE.764	*Gandy*	,,	12.12.43	Italian Navy *Altair* (1951).
DE.765	*Earl K. Olsen*	,,	13.2.44	
DE.766	*Slater*	,,	13.2.44	R.H.N. *Aetos* (1951).
DE.767	*Oswald* (*ii*)	,,	25.4.44	

Hull No.	Name	Builder	Launched	Fate
DE.768	*Ebert* (*ii*)	,,	11.5.44	R.H.N. *Ierax* (1951).
DE.769	*Neal A. Scott*	,,	4.6.44	Stricken 1/6/68 and scrapped.
DE.770	*Muir*	,,	4.6.44	South Korean Navy *Kyong Ki* (1956).
DE.771	*Sutton* (*ii*)	,,	6.8.44	South Korean Navy *Kang Won* (1956).
DE.772	*Milton Lewis* (ex-*Rogers*)	,,	6.8.44	Cancelled 1/9/44 and scrapped.
DE.773	*George M. Campbell*	,,	44	Cancelled 1/9/44 and cannibalised for spare parts.
DE.774	*Russell M. Cox*	,,	44	Cancelled 1/9/44 and scrapped.
DE.775 to DE.788	Unnamed	,,	—	Cancelled 2/10/43.

Machinery contracts: All engined by General Motors.

"Edsall" class: BLAIR, BRISTER, BROUGH, CALCATERRA, CAMP, CHAMBERS, CHATELAIN, COCKRILL, DALE W. PETERSON, DANIEL, DOUGLAS L. HOWARD, DURANT, EDSALL, FALGOUT, FARQUAR, FESSENDEN, FLAHERTY, FINCH, FISKE, FORSTER, FREDERICK C. DAVIS, FROST, HAMMANN, HARVESON, HAVERFIELD, HERBERT C. JONES, HILL, HISSEM, HOLDER, HOWARD D. CROW, HURST, HUSE, INCH, J. R. Y. BLAKELY, J. RICHARD WARD, JACOB JONES, JANSEN, JOYCE, KEITH, KIRKPATRICK, KOINER, KRETCHMER, LANSING, LEOPOLD, LOWE, MARCHAND, MARTIN H. RAY, MENGES, MERRILL, MILLS, MOORE, MOSLEY, NEUNZER, NEWELL, O'REILLY, OTTERSTETTER, PETERSON, PETTIT, PILLSBURY, POOLE, POPE, PRICE, PRIDE, RAMSDEN, RHODES, RICHEY, RICKETTS, ROBERT E. PEARY, ROY O. HALE, SAVAGE, SELLSTROM, SLOAT, SNOWDEN, STANTON, STEWART, STOCKDALE, STRICKLAND, STURTEVANT, SWASEY, SWENNING, THOMAS J. GARY, TOMICH, VANCE, WILHOITE, WILLIS.

As half designed power was now accepted for the diesel-engined destroyer escorts there was less objection to a geared drive, and with a higher rated unit available only a twin-input/single-output reduction gearbox was required for each shaft. This arrangement was therefore adopted for this class to maintain output, while the much larger radius of action of the diesel-engined vessels was a prime advantage for escort work. Twenty-one units (DE.316–325 and 382–392) were manned and operated by the United States Coast Guard for the United States Navy.

Except for the short-hulled "Evarts" class a triple bank of T.T. had been worked-in abaft the funnel in the succeeding classes. It was not always mounted, however, and when omitted generally two 20 mm. A.A. (2 × 1) guns were added, but with later vessels four 40 mm. A.A. (4 × 1) guns were substituted. In addition, the quadruple 1·1-inch A.A. mounting was subsequently replaced by a twin 40 mm. A.A. mounting in all units.

In 1945 *Camp* was re-armed with two 5-inch/38 cal. D.P. (2 × 1), twelve 40 mm. A.A. (1 × 4, 3 × 2 and 2 × 1), and six 20 mm. A.A. (6 × 1) guns, and had the T.T. removed.

When re-armed with 5-inch D.P. guns the CAMP had the Hedgehog A/S mortar resited on the superstructure deck forward together with two single 40 mm. A.A. guns in lieu of the former 3-inch and 20 mm. A.A. guns mounted forward of the bridge.

Displacement:	1,200 tons (1,490 tons full load).
Dimensions:	300(wl) 306 (oa) × 36½ × 8½ (12¼ full load) feet.
Machinery:	Two shafts; Fairbanks-Morse geared diesel engines (two/shaft) B.H.P. 6,000 = 21 knots.
Bunkers and radius:	O.F. 279 tons; 11,500 miles at 11 knots.
Armament:	Three 3-inch/50 cal. D.P. (3 × 1), two 40 mm. A.A. (1 × 2), eight 20 mm. A.A. (8 × 1) guns; three 21-inch (1 × 3) T.T.; one A/S spigot mortar (Hedgehog), eight A/S mortars, and two racks for DC's.
Complement:	186 (war 200).

Hull No.	Name	Builder	Launched	Fate
DE.129	Edsall (ii)	Consolidated Steel Corp. (Orange)	1.11.42	Stricken 1/6/68 and scrapped.
DE.130	Jacob Jones (ii)	,,	29.11.42	
DE.131	Hammann (ii) (ex-Langley)	,,	13.12.42	
DE.132	Robert E. Peary	,,	3.1.43	Sold Lipsett Inc. (Kearny) 6/9/67 and scrapped.
DE.133	Pillsbury (ii)	,,	10.1.43	DER.133 (1955); sold Boston Metals Corp. (Baltimore) ../../66 and scrapped.
DE.134	Pope (ii)	,,	12.1.43	
DE.135	Flaherty	,,	17.1.43	Sold Boston Metals Corp. (Baltimore) 4/11/66 and scrapped.
DE.136	Frederick C. Davis	,,	24.1.43	Torpedoed German submarine U.546 North Atlantic 24/4/45.

The Hedgehog A/S mortar is clearly visible abaft the fo'c'sle gun in SLOAT, and only one seaboat was carried under davits on the starboard side. A slightly taller funnel is stepped than in the diesel-engined "Evarts" class.

Hull No.	Name	Builder	Launched	Fate
DE.137	Herbert C. Jones	Consolidated Steel Corp. (Orange)	19.1.43	
DE.138	Douglas L. Howard	,,	24.1.43	
DE.139	Farquar	,,	13.2.43	
DE.140	J. R. Y. Blakely	,,	7.3.43	
DE.141	Hill	,,	28.3.43	
DE.142	Fessenden	,,	9.3.43	DER.142 (1951); stricken 1/9/66 and expended as target.
DE.143	Fiske (i)	,,	14.3.43	Torpedoed German submarine U.804 north of Azores 2/8/44.
DE.144	Frost	,,	21.3.43	Sold Peck Iron & Metal Co. (................) 29/12/66 and scrapped.

A light tripod mainmast carrying an HF/DF aerial was stepped aft on the Pope. The high bridge and the closeness of the forward guns to the stem is emphasised in this bow view.

Hull No.	Name	Builder	Launched	Fate
DE.145	Huse	Consolidated Steel Corp. (Orange)	23.3.43	
DE.146	Inch	,,	4.4.43	
DE.147	Blair	,	6.4.43	DER.147 (1957).
DE.148	Brough	,,	10.4.43	Sold Boston Metal Corp. (Baltimore) 13/10/66 and scrapped.
DE.149	Chatelain	,,	21.4.43	
DE.150	Neunzer	,,	27.4.43	
DE.151	Poole	,,	8.5.43	
DE.152	Peterson	,,	15.5.43	

Like most diesel-engined destroyer escorts the HILL *was primarily used for escort work, retained the T.T., and had an HF/DF mast fitted.*

Hull No.	Name	Builder	Launched	Fate
DE.238	*Stewart* (*ii*)	Brown Sbdg. (Houston)	22.11.42	
DE.239	*Sturtevant* (*ii*)	,,	3.12.42	DER.239 (1957).
DE.240	*Moore*	,,	21.12.42	Chinese Navy (Nationalist) .... (1969).
DE.241	*Keith* (ex-*Scott*)	,,	21.12.42	
DE.242	*Tomich*	,,	28.12.42	
DE.243	*J. Richard Ward* (ex-*James R. Ward*)	,,	6.1.43	Stricken 1/5/67 and scrapped.
DE.244	*Otterstetter*	,,	19.1.43	DER.244 (1951).
DE.245	*Sloat*	,,	21.1.43	
DE.246	*Snowden*	,,	19.2.43	Stricken 23/9/68 and scrapped.

Hull No.	Name	Builder	Launched	Fate
DE.247	*Stanton*	Brown Sbdg. (Houston)	21.2.43	
DE.248	*Swasey*	,,	18.3.43	
DE.249	*Marchand*	,,	20.3.43	
DE.250	*Hurst*	,,	14.4.43	
DE.251	*Camp*	,,	16.4.43	DER.251 (1957).
DE.252	*Howard D. Crow*	,,	26.4.43	Sold Carlton E. Ward (Beaumont) ../../70 and scrapped.
DE.253	*Pettit*	,,	28.4.43	
DE.254	*Ricketts*	,,	10.5.43	
DE.255	*Sellstrom*	,,	12.5.43	DER.255 (1956); sold Peck Iron & Metal Co. (............) ../../66 and scrapped.

Hull No.	Name	Builder	Launched	Fate
DE.316	Harveson	Consolidated Steel Corp. (Orange)	22.5.43	DER.316 (1951); stricken 1/12/66 and expended as target.
DE.317	Joyce	,,	26.5.43	DER.317 (1951).
DE.318	Kirkpatrick	,,	5.6.43	DER.318 (1951).
DE.319	Leopold	,,	12.6.43	Torpedoed German submarine U.225 south of Iceland 9/3/44, and foundered following day.
DE.320	Menges	,,	15.6.43	Torpedoed German submarine U.371 Western Mediterranean 3/5/44 and repaired with stern of Holder (DE.401)
DE.321	Mosley	,,	26.6.43	
DE.322	Newell	,,	29.6.43	U.S.C.G. (WDE.422 — 1951–54), DER.322 (1957); stricken 23/9/68 and scrapped.
DE.323	Pride	,,	3.7.43	
DE.324	Falgout	,,	24.7.43	U.S.C.G. (WDE.424 — 1951–54), DER.324 (1957).

Hull No.	Name	Builder	Launched	Fate
DE.325	*Lowe*	Consolidated Steel Corp. (Orange)	28.7.43	U.S.C.G. (1951–54 — WDE.425), DER.325 (1957); stricken 23/9/68 and scrapped.
DE.326	*Thomas J. Gary* (ex-*Gary*)	,,	21.8.43	DER.326 (1956).
DE.327	*Brister*	,,	24.8.43	DER.327 (1956); stricken 23/9/68 and scrapped.
DE.328	*Finch*	,,	28.8.43	U.S.C.G. (1951–54 — WDE.428); DER.328 (1957).
DE.329	*Kretchmer*	,,	31.8.43	DER.329 (1956).
DE 330	*O'Reilly*	,,	2.10.43	
DE.331	*Koiner*	,,	5.10.43	U.S.C.G. (1951–54 — WDE.431), DER.331 (1957); stricken 23/9/68 and scrapped.
DE.332	*Price*	,,	30.10.43	DER.332 (1956).
DE.333	*Strickland*	,,	2.11.43	DER.333 (1951).

G

Hull No.	Name	Builder	Launched	Fate
DE.334	Forster	Consolidated Steel Corp. (Orange)	13.11.43	U.S.C.G. (1951–54 — WDE.334). DER.334 (1967).
DE.335	Daniel	,,	16.11.43	
DE.336	Roy O. Hale	,,	20.11.43	DER.336 (1956).
DE.337	Dale W. Peterson	,,	22.12.43	
DE.338	Martin H. Ray	,,	29.12.43	Sold Southern Scrap Material Co., arrived New Orleans 6/5/67 for scrapping.
DE.382	Ramsden	Brown Sbdg. (Houston)	24.5.43	U.S.C.G. (1951–54 — WDE.482), DER.382 (1957).
DE.383	Mills	,,	26.5.43	DER.383 (1957).
DE.384	Rhodes	,,	29.6.43	DER.384 (1956).
DE.385	Richey	,,	30.6.43	U.S.C.G. (1951–54 — WDE.485); stricken 30/6/68 and expended.

Hull No.	Name	Builder	Launched	Fate
DE.386	*Savage*	Brown Sbdg. (Houston)	15.7.43	DER.386 (1955).
DE.387	*Vance*	,,	16.7.43	U.S.C.G. (1951–54 — WDE.487), DER.387 (1956).
DE.388	*Lansing*	,,	2.8.43	U.S.C.G. (1951–54 — WDE.488), DER.388 (1956).
DE.389	*Durant*	,,	3.8.43	U.S.C.G. (1951–54 — WDE.489), DER.389 (1956).
DE.390	*Calcaterra*	,,	16.8.43	DER.390 (1955).
DE.391	*Chambers*	,,	17.8.43	U.S.C.G. (1951–54 — WDE.491), DER.391 (1956).
DE.392	*Merrill*	,,	29.8.43	
DE.393	*Haverfield*	,,	30.8.43	DER.393 (1955); stricken 2/6/69 and scrapped.

Hull No.	Name	Builder	Launched	Fate
DE.394	*Swenning*	Brown Sbdg. (Houston)	13.9.43	
DE.395	*Willis*	,,	14.9.43	
DE.396	*Jansen*	,,	4.10.43	
DE.397	*Wilhoite*	,,	5.10.43	DER.397 (1955); stricken 2/7/69 and scrapped.
DE.398	*Cockrill*	,,	29.10.43	
DE.399	*Stockdale*	,,	30.10.43	
DE.400	*Hissem*	,,	26.12.43	DER.400 (1956).
DE.401	*Holder* (i)	,,	27.11.43	Torpedoed German aircraft off Algiers 11/4/44 and written-off as constructive total loss; scrapped in U.S.A.

Machinery contracts: All engines by Fairbanks-Morse.

"Rudderow" class: BRAY, CHAFEE, CHARLES J. KIMMEL, COATES, DANIEL A. JOY, DAY, DE LONG, EUGENE E. ELMORE, GEORGE A. JOHNSON, HODGES, HOLT, JOBB, LESLIE L. B. KNOX, LOUGH, McNULTY, METIVIER, PARLE, PEIFFER, RILEY, RUDDEROW, SUTTON, THOMAS F. NICKEL, TINSMAN, VOGELGESANG, WEEKS, WILLIAM M. WOOD, WILLIAM R. RUSH, WILLIAMS, and ONE HUNDRED & SEVENTY-FOUR unnamed vessels.

Modifications of the "Buckley" class in which the 3-inch/50 cal. guns were replaced by two 5-inch/38 cal. D.P. in single turrets fore and aft and an additional twin 40 mm. A.A. mounting forward, and the bridge and funnel were reduced in height.

Fifty units of this class were completed as fast transports (APD.87–136), and one (APD.137) was converted to this role in 1945 while the conversion of two other units (APD.138 and 139) were cancelled.

In 1945 some units had the T.T. removed so that six 40 mm. A.A. (2 × 2 and a quadruple replaced the after twin mounting) guns could be added, or a tripod mast stepped for carrying AW.RDF for duty as radar pickets.

Displacement:	1,450 tons (1,780 tons full load).
Dimensions:	300 (wl) 306 (oa) × 37 except *DE.224, 225* and *705–709* 36¾ × 9¾ (13¾ full load) feet.
Machinery:	Two Babcock & Wilcox (*DE.224 and 225*) or Combustion Engineering (*DE.230, 231, 684–686* and *706–709*) or Foster Wheeler (*DE.579–589*) boilers; two shafts; General Electric turbines and electric motors S.H.P. 12,000 = 24 except *DE.579–589* and *684–686* 23½ knots.
Bunkers and radius:	O.F. 378 tons; 5,500 miles at 15 knots.
Armament:	Two 5-inch/38 cal. D.P. (2 × 1), four 40 mm. A.A. (2 × 2), ten except *DE.684–686* eight 20 mm. A.A. (8/10 × 1) guns; three 21-inch (1 × 3) T.T.; one A/S spigot mortar (Hedgehog), eight A/S mortars, and two racks for DC's.
Complement:	186 (war 200).

Hull No.	Name	Builder	Launched	Fate
DE.224	*Rudderow*	Philadelphia N.Y.	14.10.43	Sold Nicolai Joffe Corp. (Richmond) ../../70 and scrapped.
DE.225	*Day*	,,	14.10.43	Stricken 30/6/68 and expended as target.
DE.226	*Crosley (ii)*	,,	12.2.44	APD.87 (1944); stricken ../../60 and sold-out commercially as floating power station.
DE.227	*Cread*	,,	12.2.44	APD.88 (1944); stricken ../../60 and scrapped.
DE.228	*Ruchamkin*	,,	14.6.44	APD.89 (1944), LPR.89 (1969); Colombian Navy *Cordoba* (1969).
DE.229	*Kirwin*	,,	15.6.44	APD.90 (1944) LPR.90, (1969).
DE.230	*Chaffee*	Charleston N.Y.	27.11.43	Sold .... 29/6/48 and scrapped.
DE.231	*Hodges*	,,	9.12.43	
DE.232	*Kinzer*	,,	9.12.43	APD.91 (1944); Chinese Navy (Nationalist) *Yu Shan* (1966).

The RUDDEROW *was the lead ship of the "Buckley" sub-class which were completed with a 5-inch gun armament. An additional twin 40 mm. A.A. mounting replaced the 3-inch gun forward of the bridge, and the latter was made one deck lower to reduce topweight*

Hull No.	Name	Builder	Launched	Fate
DE.233	*Register*	Charleston N.Y.	20.1.44	APD.92 (1944); Chinese Navy (Nationalist) *Tai Shan* (1966).
DE.234	*Brock*	,,	20.1.44	APD.93 (1944); stricken ../../60 and sold-out commercially as floating power station.
DE.235	*John Q. Roberts*	,,	11.2.44	APD.94 (1944); stricken ../../60 and scrapped.
DE.236	*William M. Hobby*	,,	11.2.44	APD.95 (1944); South Korean Navy *Chr Ju* (1967).
DE.237	*Ray K. Edwards*	,,	19.2.44	APD.96 (1944); stricken ../../60 and scrapped.
DE.281	*Arthur L. Bristol*	Charleston N.Y.	19.2.44	APD.97 (1944); stricken 1/4/64 and scrapped.
DE.282	*Truxtun (ii)*	,,	9.3.44	APD.98 (1944); Chinese Navy (Nationalist) *Fu Shan* (1966).
DE.283	*Upham*	,,	9.3.44	APD.99 (1944); stricken ../../60 and sold-out commercially as floating power station.
DE.284	*Vogelgesang (i)*	,,	—	Cancelled 10/6/44.
DE.285	*Weeks*	,,	—	Cancelled 10/6/44.

Some "Rudderow" class units, including the DE LONG *(above), shipped two twin 40 mm. A.A. mountings in lieu of the T.T. while a quadruple 40 mm. replaced the twin mounting aft*

Hull No.	Name	Builder	Launched	Fate
DE.286	*Sutton* (i)	Bethlehem-Hingham	—	Cancelled 12/3/44.
DE.287	*William M. Wood* (i)	,,	—	Cancelled 12/3/44.
DE.288	*William R. Rush* (i)	,,	—	Cancelled 12/3/44.
DE.289	Unnamed	,,	—	Cancelled 12/3/44.
DE.290	*Williams* (i)	,,	—	Cancelled 12/3/44.
DE.291 to DE.300	Unnamed	,,	—	Cancelled 12/3/44.
DE.579	*Riley*	Bethlehem-Hingham	29.12.43	Chinese Navy (Nationalist) *Tai Yuan* (1969).
DE.580	*Leslie L. B. Knox*	,,	8.1.44	
DE.581	*McNulty*	,,	8.1.44	
DE.582	*Metivier*	,,	12.1.44	Stricken 30/6/68 and scrapped.

A light tripod mast to carry the HF/DF aerial was stepped aft in the CHAFFEE

Hull No.	Name	Builder	Launched	Fate
DE.583	George A. Johnson	Bethlehem-Hingham	12.1.44	Sold National Metal & Steel Corp. (Terminal Island) 19/9/66; wrecked San Pedro Point 12/10/66 en-route shipbreakers, re-sold Dearborn Industrial Contractors (San Francisco) ../11/66 and scrapped.
DE.584	Charles J. Kimmel	,,	15.1.44	Stricken 30/6/68 and scrapped.
DE.585	Daniel A. Joy	,,	15.1.44	Sold North American Smelting Co. (Wilmington) ../5/66 and scrapped.
DE.586	Lough	,,	22.1.44	Sold Nicolai Joffe Corp. (Richmond) ../../70 and scrapped.
DE.587	Thomas F. Nickel	,,	22.1.44	
DE.588	Peiffer	,,	26.1.44	Expended as target off ..../5/67
DE.589	Tinsman	,,	29.1.44	
DE.590	Ringness	,,	5.2.44	APD.100 (1944), LPR. 100 (1969).
DE.591	Knudson	,,	5.2.44	APD.101 (1944), LPR.101 (1969).

Hull No.	Name	Builder	Launched	Fate
DE.592	*Rednour*	Bethlehem-Hingham	12.2.44	APD.102 (1944); Chinese Navy (Nationalist) .... (1966).
DE.593	*Tollberg*	,,	12.2.44	APD.103 (1944); Colombian Navy *Almirante Padilla* (1965).
DE.594	*William J. Pattison*	,,	15.2.44	APD.104 (1944); stricken ../../60 and scrapped.
DE.595	*Myers*	,,	15.2.44	APD.105 (1944); stricken 1/6/60 and sold-out commercially as floating power station.
DE.596	*Walter B. Cobb*	,,	23.2.44	APD.106 (1944); collision with fast transport *Gantner* off Point Sur 17/4/66 and foundered 21/4/66.
DE.597	*Earle B. Hall*	,,	1.3.44	APD.107 (1944); sold North American Smelting Co. (Wilmington) 28/1/66 and scrapped.
DE.598	*Harry L. Corl*	,,	1.3.44	APD.108 (1944); South Korean Navy *Ah San* (1966).
DE.599	*Belet*	,,	3.3.44	APD.109 (1944); Mexican Navy *California* (1964).
DE.600	*Julius A. Raven*	,,	3.3.44	APD.110 (1944); South Korean Navy *Ung Po* (1966).

Hull No.	Name	Builder	Launched	Fate
DE.601	*Walsh*	Bethlehem-Hingham	28.4.45	APD.111 (1945); sold North American Smelting Co. (Wilmington) 1/7/68 and scrapped.
DE.602	*Hunter Marshall*	,,	5.5.45	APD.112 (1945); stricken ../../60 and sold-out commercially as floating power station.
DE.603	*Earheart*	,,	12.5.45	APD.113 (1945); Mexican Navy *Papploapan* (1964).
DE.604	*Walter S. Gorka*	,,	26.5.45	APD.114 (1945); stricken ../../60 and sold-out commercially as floating power station.
DE.605	*Rogers Blood*	,,	2.6.45	APD.115 (1945); stricken ../../60 and scrapped.
DE.606	*Francovich (ii)*	,,	5.6.45	APD.116 (1945); stricken 1/4/64 and scrapped.
DE.607 to DE.616	Unnamed	,,	—	Cancelled 10/6/44.
DE.617 to DE.632	Unnamed	,,	—	Cancelled 12/8/44.
DE.645	Unnamed	,,	—	Cancelled 12/3/44.

Hull No.	Name	Builder	Launched	Fate
DE.646	Unnamed	Bethlehem-Hingham	—	Cancelled 12/3/44.
DE.647 to DE.664	Unnamed	,,	—	Cancelled 2/10/43.
DE.674	Joseph M. Auman	Consolidated Steel Corp. (Orange)	—	APD.117 (1944); Mexican Navy *Tehuantepec* (1964).
DE.684	De Long	Bethlehem (Quincy)	23.11.43	(APD.137). Expended as target ....19/2/70.
DE.685	Coates	,,	9.12.45	(APD.138). Stricken 30/1/70 and scrapped.
DE.686	Eugene E. Elmore	,,	23.12.43	Stricken 30/6/68 and scrapped.
DE.687	Kline	,,	27.6.44	APD.120 (1944); Chinese Navy (Nationalist) *Shou Shan* (1966).
DE.688	Raymon W. Herndon	,,	15.7.44	APD.121 (1944); Chinese Navy (Nationalist) *Heng Shan* (1966).
DE.689	Scribner	,,	1.8.44	APD.122 (1944); sold Gregg, Gibson & Gregg (............) 6/9/67 and scrapped.

Hull No.	Name	Builder	Launched	Fate
DE.690	Diachenko (ex-Alex Diachenko)	Bethlehem (Quincy)	15.8.44	APD.123 (1944); LPR.123 (1969).
DE.691	Horace A. Bass	,,	12.9.44	APD.124 (1944), LPR.124 (1969).
DE.692	Wantuck	,,	25.9.44	APD.125 (1944); stricken 4/3/58 (following collision) and scrapped.
DE.706	Holt	Defoe Sbdg. (Bay City)	15.2.44	South Korean Navy Chung Nam (1963).
DE.707	Jobb	,,	4.3.44	Sold Nicolai Joffe Corp. (Richmond) ../../70 and scrapped.
DE.708	Parle	,,	25.3.44	Stricken 1/7/70 and scrapped.
DE.709	Bray	,,	15.4.44	APD.139 (1945); expended as target off .... 26/3/63.
DE.710	Gosselin	,,	4.5.44	APD.126 (1944); sold National Metal & Steel Corp., arrived Terminal Island 7/4/65 for scrapping.
DE.711	Begor	,,	25.5.44	APD.127 (1944), LPR.127 (1969).

Hull No.	Name	Builder	Launched	Fate
DE.712	*Cavallaro*	Defoe Sbdg. (Bay City)	15.6.44	APD.128 (1945); South Korean Navy *Kyong Nam* (1959).
DE.713	*Donald W. Wolf*	,,	22.7.44	APD.129 (1945); Chinese Navy (Nationalist) *Hua Shan* (1968).
DE.714	*Cook*	,,	26.8.44	APD.130 (1945), LPR.130 (1969); sold National Metal and Steel Corp. (Terminal Island) ../6/70 and scrapped.
DE.715	*Walter X. Young*	,,	30.9.44	APD.131 (1945); stricken ../../62 and scrapped.
DE.716	*Balduck*	,,	27.10.44	APD.132 (1945), LPR.132 (1969).
DE.717	*Burdo*	,,	25.11.44	APD.133 (1945); sold Southern Scrap Materials Co., arrived New Orleans 6/5/67 and scrapped.
DE.718	*Kleinsmith* (ii)	,,	27.1.45	APD.134 (1945); Chinese Navy (Nationalist) *Tien Shan* (1960).
DE.719	*Weiss* (ii)	,,	17.2.45	APD.135 (1945), LPR.135 (1969).
DE.720	*Carpellotti* (ii)	,,	10.3.45	APD.136 (1945); stricken 1/12/60 and scrapped.

H

Hull No.	Name	Builder	Launched	Fate
DE.721	*Don O. Woods*	Consolidated Steel Corp. (Orange)	19.2.44	APD.118 (1945); Mexican Navy *Usumacinta* (1964).
DE.722	*Beverly W. Reid*	,,	14.3.44	APD.119 (1945), LPR.119 (1969).
DE.723	Unnamed	Dravo Corp. (Pittsburg)	—	Cancelled 12/3/44.
DE.724	Unnamed	,,	—	Cancelled 12/3/44.
DE.725 to DE.738	Unnamed	,,	—	Cancelled 2/10/43.
DE.905 to DE.959	Unnamed	Bethlehem-Hingham	—	Cancelled 15/9/43.
DE.960 to DE.995	Unnamed	Charleston N.Y.	—	Cancelled 15/9/43.
DE.996 to DE.1005	Unnamed	Defoe Sbdg. (Bay City)	—	Cancelled 15/9/43.

Machinery contracts: All engined by General Electric.

Hull No.	Name	Builder	Launched	Fate
DE.339	John C. Butler	Consolidated Steel Corp. (Orange)	11.12.43	Stricken 1/6/70 and scrapped.
DE.340	O'Flaherty	,,	14.12.43	
DE.341	Raymond	,,	8.1.44	
DE.342	Richard W. Suesens	,,	11.1.44	
DE.343	Abercrombie	,,	14.1.44	Stricken 1/5/67 and expended as target.
DE.344	Oberrender	,,	18.1.44	Bombed Japanese aircraft off Okinawa 9/5/45 and written-off as constructive total loss.
DE.345	Robert Brazier	,,	22.1.44	Stricken 1/1/68 and expended as target.
DE.346	Edwin A. Howard	,,	25.1.44	
DE.347	Jesse Rutherford	,,	29.1.44	Stricken 1/1/68 and expended as target.

"John C. Butler" class: **ABERCROMBIE, ALBERT T. HARRIS, ALFRED WOLF, ALVIN C. COCKRELL, BENNER, BIVIN, CARPELLOTTI, CECIL J. DOYLE, CHARLES E. BRANDON, CHARLES R. WARE, CHESTER T. O'BRIEN, CONKLIN, CORBESIER, CROSS, DENNIS, DENNIS J. BUCKLEY, DOUGLAS A. MUNRO, DOYLE C. BARNES, DUFILHO, EDMONDS, EDWARD H. ALLEN, EDWIN A. HOWARD, EUGENE A. GREENE, EVERETT F. LARSON, EVERSOLE, FORMOE, FRANCOVICH, FRENCH, GENTRY, GEORGE E. DAVIS, GILLIGAN, GOSS, GRADY, GROVES, GYATT, HAAS, HANNA, HAROLD J. ELLISON, HENRY W. TUCKER, HEYLIGER, HOWARD F. CLARK, JACCARD, JACK MILLER, JESSE RUTHERFORD, JOHN C. BUTLER, JOHN L. WILLIAMSON, JOHNNIE HUTCHINS, JOSEPH E. CONNOLLY, KENDALL C. CAMPBELL, KENNETH D. BAILEY, KENNETH M. WILLETT, KEPPLER, KEY, KLEINSMITH, LA PRADE, LAWRENCE C. TAYLOR, LELAND E. THOMAS, LERAY WILSON, LEWIS, LLOYD E. ACREE, LLOYD THOMAS, MACK, MAURICE J. MANUEL, McCOY REYNOLDS, McGINTY, MELVIN A. NAWMAN, MYLES C. FOX, NAIFEH, OBERRENDER, O'FLAHERTY, OLIVER MITCHELL, OSBERG, OSWALD A. POWERS, PRATT, PRESLEY, RAYMOND, RICHARD M. ROWELL, RICHARD S. BULL, RICHARD W. SUESENS, RIZZI, ROBERT BRAZIER, ROBERT F. KELLER, ROLF, ROMBACH, SAMUEL B. ROBERTS, SHEEHAN, SHELTON, SILVERSTEIN, STAFFORD, STEINAKER, STRAUS, TABBERER, THADDEUS PARKER, TRAW, TWEEDY, ULVERT M. MOORE, VANDIVIER, WAGNER, WALTER C. WANN, WALTON, WEISS, WILLIAM C. LAWE, WILLIAM SIEVERLING, WILLIAMS, WOODROW R. THOMPSON, WOODSON,** and **ONE HUNDRED and EIGHTY-FOUR** unnamed vessels.

As with the "Edsall" class the electric drive was omitted from these vessels and the turbines were coupled to the shafts through reduction gearing, and they were similarly modified as the "Rudderow" class to mount 5-inch/38 cal. D.P. guns.

Some units had the T.T. removed in 1945 so that the A.A. armament could be augmented. The construction of *Wagner* and *Vandivier* (DE.539 and 540) was suspended at the end of the war, and they were finally completed ten years later as radar pickets (DER).

The JOHN C. BUTLER, *lead ship of the class*

Displacement:	1,350 tons (1,660 tons full load).
Dimensions:	300 (wl) 306 (oa) × 36¾ × 9½ (13¼ full load) feet.
Machinery:	Two Babcock & Wilcox except *DE.339–372* and *402–424* Combustion Engineering boilers; two shafts; Westinghouse except *DE.344, 345, 348–353, 361, 364–367, 371, 372 440, 442, 445–450, 508–510* and *540* General Electric SR geared turbines S.H.P. 12,000 = 24 knots.
Bunkers and radius:	O.F. 355 tons; 5,500 miles at 15 knots.
Armament:	Two 5-inch/38 cal. D.P. (2 × 1), four 40 mm. A.A. (2 × 2) and ten 20 mm. A.A. (10 × 1) except *DE.448–450* and *510* four 40 mm. A.A.(1 × 4) and sixteen 20 mm. A.A. (3 × 2 and 10 × 1) and *DE.537* and *538* ten 40 mm. A.A. (1 × 4 and 3 × 2) and ten 20 mm. A.A. (10 × 1) guns; three except *DE.371, 372, 448–450, 510, 537* and *538* nil 21-inch (1 × 3) T.T.; one A/S spigot mortar, (Hedgehog), eight A/S mortars, and two racks for DC's.
Complement:	186 (war 200).

Hull No.	Name	Builder	Launched	Fate
DE.348	*Key*	Consolidated Steel Corp. (Orange)	12.2.44	
DE.349	*Gentry*	,,	15.2.44	
DE.350	*Traw*	,,	12.2.44	Expended as target off .... 17/8/68.
DE.351	*Maurice J. Manuel*	,,	19.2.44	Stricken 1/5/66 and expended as target.
DE.352	*Naifeh*	,,	29.2.44	Expended as target off San Nicolas Island 13/7/66.
DE.353	*Doyle C. Barnes*	,,	4.3.44	
DE.354	*Kenneth M. Willett*	,,	7.3.44	
DE.355	*Jaccard*	,,	18.3.44	Stricken 1/11/67 and expended as target.
DE.356	*Lloyd E. Acree*	,,	21.3.44	

Near broadside view of the ROBERT BRAZIER *showing generally cluttered appearance of upperworks and inconspicuous funnel*

Hull No.	Name	Builder	Launched	Fate
DE.357	*George E. Davis*	Consolidated Steel Corp. (Orange)	8.4.44	
DE.358	*Mack*	,,	11.4.44	
DE.359	*Woodson*	,,	29.4.44	Sold Boston Metals Corp. (Baltimore) 16/8/66 and scrapped.
DE.360	*Johnnie Hutchins*	,,	2.5.44	
DE.361	*Walton*	,,	20.5.44	Stricken 23/9/68 and scrapped.
DE.362	*Rolf*	,,	23.5.44	
DE.363	*Pratt*	,,	1.6.44	
DE.364	*Rombach*	,,	6.6.44	
DE.365	*McGinty*	,,	5.8.44	Stricken 23/9/68 and scrapped.

As completed the Cross *lacked T.T. and later had the light A.A. armament augmented*

Hull No.	Name	Builder	Launched	Fate
DE.366	*Alvin C. Cockrell*	Consolidated Steel Corp. (Orange)	8.8.44	Stricken 23/9/68 and scrapped.
DE.367	*French*	,,	17.6.44	
DE.368	*Cecil J. Doyle*	,,	1.7.44	Stricken 1/8/67 and expended as target.
DE.369	*Thaddeus Parker*	,,	26.8.44	Sold Peck Iron & Metal Co. (..........) 9/7/68 and scrapped.
DE.370	*John L. Williamson*	,,	29.8.44	Stricken 15/9/70 and scrapped.
DE.371	*Presley*	,,	19.8.44	Sold National Metal & Steel Corp. (Terminal Island) ../4/70 and scrapped.
DE.372	*Williams (ii)*	,,	22.8.44	Stricken 1/8/67 and expended as target.
DE.373	*William C. Lawe (ii)*	,,	—	Cancelled 6/6/44.
DE.374	*Lloyd Thomas (ii)*	,,	—	Cancelled 6/6/44.

Two twin 40 mm. mountings have been added amidships in lieu of the T.T. in the HANNA

Hull No.	Name	Builder	Launched	Fate
DE.375	Keppler (ii)	Consolidated Steel Corp. (Orange)	—	Cancelled 6/6/44.
DE.376	Kleinsmith (i)	,,	—	Cancelled 6/6/44.
DE.377	Henry W. Tucker (i)	,,	—	Cancelled 6/6/44.
DE.378	Weiss (i)	,,	—	Cancelled 6/6/44.
DE.379	Francovich (i)	,,	—	Cancelled 6/6/44.
DE.380	Unnamed	,,	—	Cancelled 6/6/44.
DE.381	Unnamed	,,	—	Cancelled 6/6/44.
DE.402	Richard S. Bull	Brown Sbdg. (Houston)	16.11.43	Stricken 30/6/68 and scrapped.
DE.403	Richard M. Rowell	,,	17.11.43	Stricken 30/6/68 and scrapped.

The HEYLIGER *also had a strengthened light A.A. armament in lieu of the T.T. and could put up a volume of A.A. fire little inferior to a fleet destroyer*

Hull No.	Name	Builder	Launched	Fate
DE.404	Eversole (i)	Brown Sbdg. (Houston)	3.12.43	Torpedoed I.J.N. submarine *I.45* east of Leyte 28/10/44.
DE.405	Dennis	,,	4.12.43	
DE.406	Edmonds	,,	17.12.43	
DE.407	Shelton (i)	,,	18.12.43	Torpedoed I.J.N. submarine *RO.41* off Morotai 3/10/44.
DE.408	Strauss	,,	30.12.43	Stricken 1/5/66 and expended as target.
DE.409	La Prade	,,	31.12.43	
DE.410	Jack Miller		10.1.44	Stricken 30/6/68 and scrapped.
DE.411	Stafford	,,	11.1.44	
DE.412	Walter C. Wann	,,	19.1.44	Stricken 30/6/68 and scrapped.

There was little external distinction between the "Rudderow" and "John C. Butler" classes except that the latter were completed with a quadruple 40 mm. A.A. mounting aft as shown in this view of HOWARD F. CLARK

Hull No.	Name	Builder	Launched	Fate
DE.413	Samuel B. Roberts (i)	Brown Sbdg. (Houston)	20.1.44	Gunfire I.J.N. warships off Samar 25/10/44.
DE.414	LeRay Wilson	,,	28.1.44	
DE.415	Lawrence C. Taylor	,,	29.1.44	
DE.416	Melvin R. Nawman	,,	7.2.44	
DE.417	Oliver Mitchell	,,	8.2.44	
DE.418	Tabberer	,,	18.2.44	
DE.419	Robert F. Keller	,,	19.2.44	
DE.420	Leland E. Thomas	,,	28.2.44	
DE.421	Chester T. O'Brien	,,	29.2.44	

Bow view of the HOWARD F. CLARK. As only one seaboat was carried under davits on the port side abaft the bridge, the 40 mm. gun pit abreast the funnel had to be positioned higher than the corresponding one on the other side to clear the davit head.

Hull No.	Name	Builder	Launched	Fate
DE.422	*Douglas A. Munro*	Brown Sbdg. (Houston)	8.3.44	Stricken 1/12/65 and expended as target.
DE.423	*Dufilho*	,,	9.3.44	
DE.424	*Haas*	,,	20.3.44	Sold Gregg, Gibson & Gregg (..........) 6/9/67 and scrapped.
DE.425 to DE.437	Unnamed	Boston N.Y.	—	Cancelled 13/3/44.
DE.438	*Corbesier (ii)*	Federal Sbdg. (Kearny)	13.2.44	
DE.439	*Conklin*	,,	13.2.44	Stricken 1/10/70 and scrapped.
DE.440	*McCoy Reynolds*	,,	22.2.44	Portuguese Navy *Corte Real* (1957).
DE.441	*William Sieverling*	,,	7.3.44	
DE.442	*Ulvert M. Moore*	,,	7.3.44	Expended as target off .... 15/7/66.

Hull No.	Name	Builder	Launched	Fate
DE.443	Kendall C. Campbell	Federal Sbdg. (Kearny)	19.3.44	
DE.444	Goss	,,	19.3.44	
DE.445	Grady	,,	2.4.44	Stricken 30/6/68 and scrapped.
DE.446	Charles E. Brannon	,,	23.4.44	Stricken 23/9/68 and scrapped.
DE.447	Albert T. Harris	,,	16.4.44	Stricken 23/9/68 and scrapped.
DE.448	Cross	,,	4.7.44	Sold Southern Scrap Materials Co. arrived New Orleans 8/4/68 for scrapping.
DE.449	Hanna	,,	4.7.44	
DE.450	Joseph E. Connolly	,,	6.8.44	Stricken 1/6/70 and scrapped.
DE.451	Woodrow R. Thompson (i)	,,	—	Cancelled 6/6/44.

Completed post-war as radar pickets the VANDIVIER (*above*) *and the* WAGNER (*right*) *had the super-structure extended out to the side and were rigged with tripod masts to carry more extensive RDF aerials. They were armed with two 5-inch D.P. guns and a Hedgehog ATW.*

Hull No.	Name	Builder	Launched	Fate
DE.452	*Steinaker* (*i*)	Federal Sbdg. (Kearny)	—	Cancelled 6/6/44.
DE.453 to DE.456	Unnamed	,,	—	Cancelled 6/6/44.
DE.457 to DE.477	Unnamed	,,	—	Cancelled 12/3/44.
DE.478 to DE.507	Unnamed	,,	—	Cancelled 2/10/43.
DE.508	*Gilligan* (ex-*Donaldson*)	,,	22.2.44	
DE.509	*Formoe* (*ii*)	,,	2.4.44	Portuguese Navy *Diogo Cao* (1957).
DE.510	*Heyliger*	,,	6.8.44	Stricken 1/5/66 and scrapped.
DE.511	Unnamed	,,	—	Cancelled 6/6/44.
DE.512 to DE.515	Unnamed	,,	—	Cancelled 12/3/44.

Hull No.	Name	Builder	Launched	Fate
DE.531	Edward H. Allen	Boston N.Y.	7.10.43	
DE.532	Tweedy	,,	7.10.43	Expended as target .... 30/6/69.
DE.533	Howard F. Clark	,,	8.11.43	
DE.534	Silverstein	,,	8.11.43	
DE.535	Lewis	,,	7.12.43	Stricken 1/1/66 and expended as target.
DE.536	Bivin	,,	7.12.43	Stricken 30/6/68 and scrapped.
DE.537	Rizzi	,,	7.12.43	
DE.538	Osberg	,,	7.12.43	
DE.539	Wagner	,,	27.12.43	Construction suspended 1946–54, DER.539 (1955).
DE.540	Vandivier	,,	27.12.43	Construction suspended 1946–54, DER.540 (1955).

Hull No.	Name	Builder	Launched	Fate
DE.541	Sheehan	Boston N.Y.	27.12.43	Cancelled 7/1/46 and scrapped.
DE.542	Oswald A. Powers	,,	27.12.43	Cancelled 7/1/46 and scrapped.
DE.543	Groves	,,	44	Cancelled 5/9/44 and scrapped.
DE.544	Alfred Wolf	,,	44	Cancelled 5/9/44 and scrapped.
DE.545	Harold J. Ellison (i)	,,	—	Cancelled 10/6/44.
DE.546	Myles C. Fox (i	,,	—	Cancelled 10/6/44.
DE.547	Charles R. Ware (i)	,,	—	Cancelled 10/6/44.
DE.548	Carpellotti (i)	,,	—	Cancelled 10/6/44.
DE.549	Eugene A. Greene (i)	,,	—	Cancelled 10/6/44.
DE.550	Gyatt (i)	,,	—	Cancelled 10/6/44.
DE.551	Benner (i)	,,	—	Cancelled 10/6/44.
DE.552	Kenneth D. Bailey (i)	,,	—	Cancelled 10/6/44.
DE.553	Dennis J. Buckley (i)	,,	—	Cancelled 10/6/44.

Hull No.	Name	Builder	Launched	Fate
DE.554	*Everett F. Larson (i)*	Boston N.Y.	—	Cancelled 10/6/44.
DE.555 to DE.562	Unnamed	,,	—	Cancelled 10/6/44.
DE.801 to DE.832	Unnamed	Boston N.Y.	—	Cancelled 15/9/43.
DE.833 to DE.840	Unnamed	Mare Island N.Y. (Vallejo)	—	Cancelled 15/9/43.
DE.841 to DE.872	Unnamed	Brown Sbdg. (Houston)	—	Cancelled 15/9/43.
DE.873 to DE.886	Unnamed	Dravo Corp. (Wilmington)	—	Cancelled 15/9/43.
DE.887 to DE.898	Unnamed	Western Pipe (San Pedro)	—	Cancelled 15/9/43.
DE.899 to DE.904	Unnamed	Federal Sbdg. (Newark)	—	Cancelled 15/9/43.

Machinery contracts: *DE.344, 345, 348–353, 361, 364–367, 371, 372, 440, 442, 445–450, 508–510* and *540* engined by General Electric; and all others by Westinghouse.

Analysis of war losses

AIR ATTACK		SURFACE ATTACK		SUBMARINE ATTACK	
bomb	*torpedo*	*gunfire*	*torpedo*	*torpedo*	*mine*
Ward	Hovey**	Edsall	Blue	Jacob Jones	Sturtevant
Dickerson		Pope†	Benham	Leary	Montgomery*
Herbert	Lansdale	Pillsbury	Rowan	Rueben James	Percy**
Peary	Meredith (i)		Walke		
Brooks	Beatty	Cushing	Gwin	Porter	Tucker
Barry		Preston	Barton	Henley	Corry
Gamble*	Twiggs	Monssen		Hammann	Glennon
Palmer**		Laffey	Chevalier	O'Brien	
Long**	Holder	Duncan	Cooper	Buck	Halligan
				Bristol	Meredith (ii)‡
Mahan		Hoel		Strong	
Reid		Johnston			Rich
Jarvis				Donnell	
Sims		Samuel B.		Fechteler	
Morris		Roberts		Underhill	
Emmons**				Frederick C.	
Forrest				Davis	
Aaron Ward (i)				Fiske	
Maddox				Leopold	
Harding				Eversole	
Butler				Shelton	

bomb	torpedo	gunfire	torpedo	torpedo	mine
Shubrick					
De Haven					
Hutchins					
Pringle					
Leutze					
Thatcher					
Brownson					
Luce					
Abner Read					
Bush		*MISCELLANEOUS CAUSES*			

	bomb	foundered	collision	wrecked	explosion
Evans					
Haggard					
Morrison					
William D. Porter	J. William Ditter*	Borie	Parrott	Truxton	Stewart††
Newcomb	Aaron Ward (ii)*	Hull	Noa	Dorsey	Wasmuth
Callaghan	Hugh W. Hadley	Monaghan	Perkins	Southard	Turner
Colquoun		Warrington	Ingraham	Worden	
Little		Spence		Shaw	
Mannert L. Abele	England		Whitehurst		
Drexler	Oberrender			Longshaw	

* DM conversion; ** DMS conversion; † loss caused by gunfire and bombing; ‡ loss caused by mining and bombing; †† blown-up and scuttled to prevent capture.

Summary of war losses

Cause	Destroyers	Destroyer escorts	Total
Bomb	44	2	46
(air)	5	1	6
Torpedo (surface)	6	2	8
(submarine)	10	8	18
Gunfire	$9\frac{1}{2}$	1	$10\frac{1}{2}$
Mine	$7\frac{1}{2}$	1	$8\frac{1}{2}$
Miscellaneous	17	2	19
Totals	99	17	116

The SELFRIDGE *with temporary bow makes Mare Island Navy Yard for repair.*

K

Fessenden	(DE–142) II/86, 87, 90	
Fieberling	(DE–640) II/44, 45, 66	
Finch	(DE–328) II/86, 87, 97	
Finnegan	(DE–307) II/28, 29, 41	
Fiske(i)	(DE–143) II/86, 87, 90	
Fiske(ii)	(DD–842) II/3–5, 18	
Fitch	(DD–462) I/87–89, 91	
Flaherty	(DE–135) II/86–88	
Fleming(i)	(DE–271) II/28, 29, 32	
Fleming(ii)	(DE–32) II/28, 29, 34	
Fletcher	(DD–445) I/105–110	
Floyd B. Parkes	(DD–884) II/3–5, 24	
Flusser	(DD–368) I/54–56	
Fogg	(DE–57) II/44–46	
Foote	(DD–511) I/105–109,116	
Foreman	(DE–633) II/44, 45, 65	
Formoe(i)	(DE–58) II/44–46	
Formoe(ii)	(DE–509) II/116, 117, 134	
Forrest	(DD–461) I/87–89, 91	
Forrest Royal	(DD–872) II/3–5, 22	
Forster	(DE–334) II/86, 87, 98	
Foss	(DE–59) II/44, 45, 48	
Fowler	(DE–222) II/44, 45, 63	
Fox	(DD–234) I/22–24	
Frament	(DE–677) II/44, 45, 68	
Francis M. Robinson	(DD–220) II/44, 45, 62	
Francovich(i)	(DE–379) II/116, 117, 124	
Francovich(ii)	(DE–606) II/101, 110	
Frank E. Evans	(DD–754) I/144, 145, 152	
Frank Knox	(DD–742) II/3–5, 8	
Frankford	(DD–497) I/87–89, 94	

Franks	(DD–554) I/105–109, 124	
Frazier	(DD–607) I/87–89, 95	
Fred T. Berry	(DD–858) II/3–5, 20	
Frederick C. Davis	(DE–136) II/86–88	
French	(DE–367) II/116, 117, 122	
Frost	(DE–144) II/86, 87, 90	
Frybarger	(DE–705) II/44, 45, 70	
Fullam	(DD–474) I/105–109, 112	
Furse	(DD–882) II/3–5, 24	

G

Gainard	(DD–706) I/144–146	
Gamble	(DM–15) I/32–34	
Gandy	(DE–764) II/73, 84	
Gansevoort	(DD–608) II/87–89, 98	
Gantner	(DE–60) II/44, 45, 48	
Garfield Thomas	(DE–193) II/73, 81	
Gary	(DE–61) II/44, 45, 48	
Gatling	(DD–671) I/130, 131, 136	
Gaynier	(DE–751) II/73, 83	
Gearing	(DD–710) II/3–6	
Gendreau	(DE–639) II/44, 45, 66	
Gentry	(DE–349) II/116–118	
George(i)	(DE–276) II/28, 29, 39	
George(ii)	(DE–697) II/44, 45, 69	
George A. Johnson	(DE–583) II/101, 108	
George E. Davis	(DE–357) II/116, 117, 120	
George K. MacKenzie	(DD–836) II/3–5, 16	
George M. Campbell	(DE–773) II/73, 85	
George W. Ingram	(DE–62) II/44, 45, 48	

Hart	(DD–594)	I/105–109, 128
Harveson	(DE–316)	I/86, 87, 96
Harwood	(DD–861)	II/3–5, 20
Hatfield	(DD–231)	I/22–24
Haverfield	(DE–393)	II/86, 87, 99
Hawkins	(DD–873)	II/3–5, 22
Haynsworth	(DD–700)	I/143–145
Hayter	(DE–212)	II/44, 45, 61
Hazelwood	(DD–531)	I/105–109, 120
Healy	(DD–672)	I/130, 131, 136
Heermann	(DD–532)	I/105–109, 120
Helm	(DD–388)	I/60–64
Hemminger	(DE–746)	I/73, 83
Henderson	(DD–785)	II/3–5, 10
Henley(i)	(DD–391)	I/60–64
Henley(ii)	(DD–762)	I/144, 145, 152
Henry A. Wiley	(DD–749)	I/144, 145, 150
Henry R. Kenyon	(DE–683)	II/44, 45, 68
Henry W. Tucker(i)	(DE–377)	II/116, 117, 124
Henry W. Tucker(ii)	(DD–875)	II/3–5, 22
Herbert	(DD–160)	I/12, 13, 20
Herbert C. Jones	(DE–137)	II/86, 87, 90
Herbert J. Thomas	(DD–833)	II/3–5, 16
Herndon	(DD–638)	I/87, 89, 102
Herzog(i)	(DE–277)	II/28, 29, 39
Herzog(ii)	(DE–178)	II/73, 80
Heyliger	(DE–510)	II/116, 117, 134
Heywood L. Edwards	(DD–663)	I/130, 131, 134
Hickox	(DD–673)	I/130, 131, 136
Higbee	(DD–806)	II/3–5, 12
Hilary P. Jones	(DD–427)	I/78–80
Hilbert	(DE–742)	II/73, 82
Hill	(DE–141)	II/86, 87, 90
Hissem	(DE–400)	II/86, 87, 100
Hobby	(DD–610)	I/87–89, 98
Hobson	(DD–464)	I/87–89, 91
Hodges	(DE–231)	II/101, 102
Hoel(i)	(DD–533)	I/105–109,120
Hoel(ii)	(DD–768)	II/3–5, 8
Hogan	(DMS–6)	I/32, 33, 35
Holder(i)	(DE–401)	I/86, 87, 100
Holder(ii)	(DD–819)	II/3–5, 14
Hollis	(DE–794)	II/44, 45, 71
Hollister	(DD–788)	II/3–5, 10
Holt	(DE–706)	II/101, 112
Holton	(DE–703)	II/44, 45, 70
Hopewell	(DD–681)	I/130, 131, 138
Hopkins	(DMS–13)	I/32, 33, 38
Hopping	(DE–155)	II/44, 45, 58
Horace A. Bass	(DE–691)	II/101, 112
Hovey	(DMS–11)	I/32, 33, 38
Howard	(DMS–7)	I/32, 33, 35
Howard D. Crow	(DE–252)	II/86, 87, 95
Howard F. Clark	(DE–533)	II/116, 117, 135
Howorth	(DD–592)	I/105–109, 128
Hudson	(DD–475)	I/105–109, 112
Hugh Purvis	(DD–709)	I/144–146
Hugh W. Hadley	(DD–774)	I/144, 145, 154
Hughes	(DD–410)	I/76–78
Hull	(DD–350)	I/43–45
Humphreys	(DD–236)	I/22–24
Hunt	(DD–674)	I/130, 131, 136

Martin H. Ray	(DE–338) II/86, 87, 98	
Marts	(DE–174) II/73, 78	
Mason	(DE–529) II/28, 29, 43	
Massey	(DD–778) I/144, 145, 154	
Maurice J. Manuel	(DE–351) II/116–118	
Maury	(DD–401) I/60–64	
Mayo	(DD–422) I/78–80	
Mayrant	(DD–402) I/60–64	
McAnn(i)	(DE–73) II/44, 45, 60	
McAnn(ii)	(DE–179) II/73, 80	
McCaffery	(DD–860) II/3–5, 20	
McCall	(DD–400) I/60–64	
McCalla	(DD–488) I/87–89, 94	
McClelland	(DE–750) II/73, 83	
McConnell	(DE–163) II/73, 76	
McCook	(DD–496) I/87–89, 94	
McCord	(DD–534) I/105–109, 120	
McCormick	(DD–223) I/22–24	
McCoy Reynolds	(DE–440) II/116, 117, 130	
McDermut	(DD–677) I/130, 131, 138	
McDougal	(DD–358) I/45–47	
McGinty	(DE–365) II/116, 117, 120	
McGowan	(DD–678) I/130, 131, 138	
McKean	(DD–784) II/3–5, 20	
McKee	(DD–575) I/105–109, 126	
McLanahan	(DD–615) I/87–89, 98	
McNair	(DD–679) I/130, 131, 138	
McNulty	(DE–581) II/101, 106	
Meade	(DD–602) I/87–89, 95	
Melvin	(DD–680) I/130, 131, 138	
Melvin R. Nawman	(DE–416) II/116, 117, 128	

Menges	(DE–320) II/86, 87, 96	
Meredith(i)	(DD–434) I/78, 79, 82	
Meredith(ii)	(DD–726) II/144–146	
Meredith(iii)	(DD–890) II/3–5, 25	
Merrill	(DE–392) II/86, 87, 99	
Mertz	(DD–691) I/130, 131, 140	
Mervine	(DD–489) I/87–89, 94	
Metcalf	(DD–595) I/105–109, 128	
Metivier	(DE–582) II/101, 106	
Micka	(DE–176) II/73, 78	
Miller	(DD–535) I/105–109, 120	
Mills	(DE–383) II/86, 87, 98	
Milton Lewis	(DE–772) II/73, 85	
Mitchell	(DE–43) II/28, 29, 36	
Moale	(DD–693) I/143–145	
Moffet	(DD–362) I/45–47	
Monaghan	(DD–354) I/43–45	
Monssen(i)	(DD–436) I/78, 79, 82	
Monssen(ii)	(DD–798) I/130, 131, 140	
Montgomery	(DM–17) I/32–34	
Moore	(DE–240) II/86, 87, 94	
Morris	(DD–417) I/76–78	
Morrison	(DD–560) I/105–109, 125	
Mosley	(DE–321) II/86, 87, 96	
Mugford	(DD–389) I/60–64	
Muir	(DE–770) II/73, 85	
Mullany	(DD–528) I/105–109, 120	
Murphy	(DD–603) I/87–89, 95	
Murray	(DD–576) I/105–109, 126	
Mustin	(DD–413) I/76–78	
Myles, C. Fox(i)	(DE–546) II/116, 117, 136	

154

157